ブータン王国第4代国王王女ケサン・チョデン・ワンチュック殿下
写真：ブータン王国提供

龍谷大学大宮学舎。本学は1639（寛永16）年に設立された。

左から三谷真澄、鍋島直樹、桂紹隆、ケサン王女殿下、V・ナムギャル、カルマ・ツェーテム。
2011年2月14日、龍谷大学。

Googleマップより

ブータン王国 Image©2006 TerraMetrics, ©2006 Europa Technologies

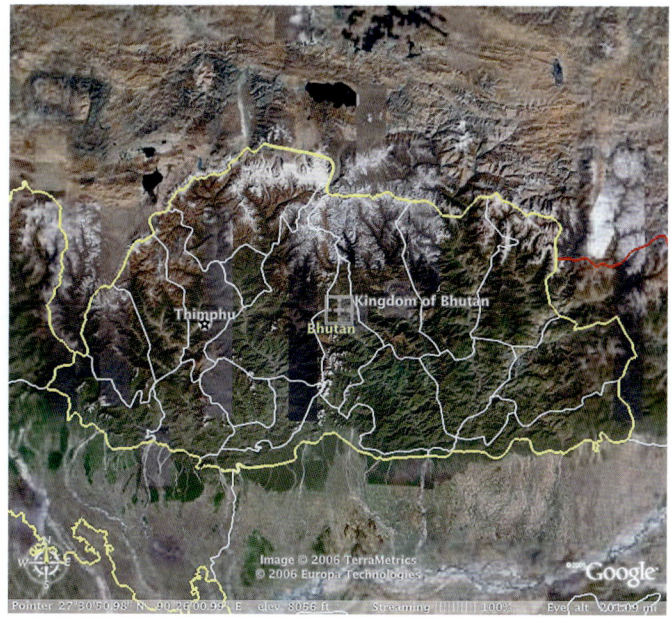

南アジア中の位置 Image©2006 NASA, Image©2006 TerraMetrics, Colomb©2006 Europa Technologies

キチュラカンでマニ車をまわす女性。マニ車を右回りに回転させると仏典を読誦したのと同じ功徳があると信じられている。　以下の写真撮影：三谷真澄

キチュラカン内部。キチュラカンは、ブータン最古の寺院として知られている。

パロ・ゾン遠景。ゾンは、ブータン各地の政治的中枢機関と寺院機能を併せ持つ施設である。

プナカゾン遠景。プナカは、かつての冬の首都であった。

パロ空港全景。

峠ではためく無数のダルシン(経文旗)。

ケサン王女殿下特別講演

ブータン王国の国民総幸福(GNH)政策
―仏教思想はどのように活かされるか―

THE GROSS NATIONAL HAPPINESS POLICY OF THE KINGDOM OF BHUTAN: TURNING BUDDHIST THOUGHT INTO REALITY

A SPECIAL LECTURE BY HER ROYAL HIGHNESS PRINCESS KESANG CHODEN WANGCHUCK

The National Emblem of the Kingdom of Bhutan

龍谷大学 アジア仏教文化研究センター
Research Center for Buddhist Cultures in Asia, Ryukoku University

龍谷大学 人間・科学・宗教オープン・リサーチ・センター
Open Research Center for Humanities, Science and Religion, Ryukoku University

ケ サ ン 王 女 殿 下 特 別 講 演
ブータン王国の国民総幸福（GNH）政策
－仏教思想はどのように活かされるか－

－ 目　次 －

謝　辞 *1*

開会の辞 *2*
　若原　道昭（筑紫女学園大学学長・龍谷大学第17代学長）

特別講演 *5*
　ケサン・チョデン・ワンチュック王女殿下
　「国民総幸福（GNH）政策：ブータン王国の開発の理念」

パネルディスカッション *19*
　Ｖ．ナムギャル（ブータン王国大使）
　カルマ・ツェテーム（GNH委員会長官）
　桂　紹隆
　（龍谷大学アジア仏教文化研究センター長・文学部教授）
　鍋島　直樹
　（龍谷大学人間・科学・宗教オープン・リサーチ・センター長・文学部教授）

　コーディネーター
　三谷　真澄（龍谷大学国際文化学部教授）

閉会の辞 *35*
　赤松　徹眞（現龍谷大学第18代学長・文学部教授）

ブータン王国について *37*
　参考文献

おわりに～編集後記 *45*

The Gross National Happiness Policy of the Kingdom of Bhutan : Turning Buddhist Thought into Reality

A Special Lecture by Her Royal Highness Princess Kesang Choden Wangchuck

— Contents —

Acknowledgements 47

Opening Address 49
- Dosho Wakahara, President of Chikushi Jogakuen University, 17th President of Ryukoku University

Special Lecture 51
- H.R.H. Princess Kesang Choden Wangchuck, the Kingdom of Bhutan
  "On Gross National Happiness: Bhutan's Development Philosophy"

Panel Discussion 66
- V. Namgyel, Ambassador of Bhutan
- Karma Tshiteem, Secretary, Gross National Happiness Commission
- Shoryu Katsura, Director of the Research Center for Buddhist Cultures in Asia, Professor, Faculty of Letters, Ryukoku University
- Naoki Nabeshima, Director of the Open Research Center for Humanities, Science and Religion, Professor, Faculty of Letters, Ryukoku University

  Coordinator
  - Mazumi Mitani, Professor, Faculty of Intercultural Communication, Ryukoku University

Closing Address 85
- Tesshin Akamatsu, Professor, Faculty of Letters, 18th President of Ryukoku University

Postscript 89

謝　辞

　ブータン王国のケサン・チョデン・ワンチュック王女殿下は、2011年2月に「ＫＹＯＴＯ地球環境の殿堂」の受賞者の一人として選ばれた、お父上、ジクメ・センゲ・ワンチュック前国王のご名代として初来日されました。この機会に龍谷大学にお招きして、ブータン王国の「国民総幸福」(GNH) 政策についてご講演いただきました。本書は、ケサン王女殿下のご講演『国民総幸福(GNH) 政策：ブータン王国の開発の理念』をはじめ、開会・閉会の辞や講演後のパネル・ディスカッションをも含めて、当日の模様を最大限忠実に再現したものです。

　素晴らしいご講演をして頂いたケサン王女殿下、パネル・ディスカッションに加わっていただいたブータン王国大使ナムギャル閣下とGNH委員会長官カルマ・ツェテーム氏には衷心よりお礼申し上げます。

　本書を日英両語で出版いたしますのは、日本の読者だけでなく、世界の人々にブータン王国のGNH政策の成果をお伝えし、21世紀の地球が直面している諸問題を解決するための一つの指針を示したいと思うからです。

　2011年3月11日に発生した東日本大震災に際し、ブータン王国をはじめ、世界中の国々から、心温まる支援をいただきましたことを深く感謝いたします。世界の危機や困難に際して、このブータン王国のGNH政策がいかに重要であるかを本書を通じて考えていただけたら幸いです。

　最後に、本書の刊行にご理解を頂いたブータン王国の関係者各位と京都環境文化学術フォーラム、さらにケサン王女殿下来学のご縁を結んで頂きました龍谷大学政策学部 富野暉一郎教授に心よりお礼申し上げます。

ナミサミ・カディンチェラ
合掌

龍谷大学アジア仏教文化研究センター長　桂　紹隆
龍谷大学人間・科学・宗教オープン・リサーチ・センター長　鍋島直樹

開幕挨拶

筑紫女学園大学学長・龍谷大学第17代学長
若原 道昭

　ブータン王国と日本との国交樹立25周年にあたる今年、ケサン・チョデン・ワンチュック王女殿下をお招きして本学でご講演を賜わりますことは誠に光栄なことです。ブータン王国は、世界有数の仏教王国であり、2008年に立憲君主制に移行し、男女平等や情報政策の推進など民主化と近代化を強力に進めておられます。

　ブータン王国は、1980年代から、国民総生産ではなく、仏教思想に基づく国民総幸福の理念と政策を導入し、国民の幸福とともに人と自然の調和を尊重し、世界に向って新しい国のあり方を示しています。

　ケサン王女殿下は、国民総幸福センターの創立者でもあるとおうかがいしています。本日のご講演では、ケサン王女殿下より直接にGNH政策についてお話をうかがう機会をいただき、心から感謝申し上げます。ブータン王国のナムギャル大使によれば、ブータン王国は仏教の心によりながら、経済的な成長と精神的な幸福とのバランスをはかっておられます。

　科学技術それ自身は、本質的に自らの意思をもっていません。何らかの目

的を持って科学技術を制御するのは人間です。人間の欲望には際限がありません。人間の欲望を制御するのは宗教です。そのような視点から、本学では人間・科学・宗教の融合を掲げてきました。本学は親鸞聖人の精神に基づき創設された、創立370年余の歴史をもち仏教研究にも長い伝統を有しています。その中でも、人間・科学・宗教オープン・リサーチ・センターとアジア仏教文化研究センターは、文部科学省私立大学戦略的研究基盤形成支援事業に採択された大型研究プロジェクトです。本講演会はこれら二つの研究センターの主催によって実現したものであり、学術的な真価を広く世界と共有することを願っています。

　さまざまな困難の中で、本講演会の開催のためにご尽力いただいた関係者すべての方々に厚く御礼申し上げます。仏教を建学の精神として掲げる龍谷大学にとって、ブータン王国のケサン王女殿下の記念講演は、本学にふさわしいご縁であり、皆様がともに豊かな実りを感じ取っていただけることを念願します。重ねてケサン王女殿下に御礼申し上げます。

特別講演

ブータン王国
ケサン・チョデン・ワンチュック王女殿下

「国民総幸福（GNH）政策：ブータン王国の開発の理念」

2011年2月14日、龍谷大学において特別講演をされるケサン・チョデン・ワンチュック王女殿下

講師紹介

1982年生まれ。ブータン王国の第4代国王陛下ジクメ・センゲ・ワンチュック前国王の第4女、現国王ジクメ・ケサル・ナムギャル・ワンチュック国王陛下の妹君。
ブータンの公立高校を経て、米国スタンフォード大学で心理学の学位を取得。2007年、国王によってブータン中心地域の人民福祉事業の国王代理に任命される。ブムタン県を拠点とされ、住民への福祉（キドゥ）事業の効果的な取組を進められている。苦楽をともにすることを意味するキドゥは、主要開発事業から取り残された弱い立場の人々に対して支援を施すという国王の伝統的な公務である。
王女は、ブータン王国のすみずみまで行脚し、困窮している人々を調査される一方、人々の声に耳を傾け、彼らと生活をともにされている。
国民総幸福の考えを国内外で普及することに積極的に取り組まれており、ブータン中部のブムタン県に建設される幸福のための国民総幸福センターの創立者でもある。

ケサン・チョデン・ワンチュック王女殿下
特別講演「国民総幸福(GNH) 政策：ブータン王国の開発の理念」

　本日、ブータン国王、ジグメ・ケサル・ナムギャル・ワンチュック陛下の、心からのご挨拶を皆様にお届けできるのは、私にとって名誉であり、喜びでもあります。また、父ジグメ・センゲ・ワンチュック前国王から、日本の皆様の幸福を願うメッセージをたずさえて来たことは、光栄です。私の家族もブータン王国の国民も、皆様のすばらしい日本が、技術革新と勤勉と類い稀な協調の精神によって、最高レベルの経済的繁栄を達成したことに、常に尊敬の念をもってまいりました。独自の文化を持ち、平和を愛する国として、日本は世界の国々に感銘を与えています。日本を初めて訪問し、父がブータン王国を意味のある変革の軌道に乗せるために構想した国民総幸福（GHN）という考えを皆様と共有できますことを心からうれしく思います。私たちは、皆様が国民総幸福という考え方に関心を示されていることにとても勇気づけられます。そしてそれは、ブータン王国の開発の経験がより大きな世界にも適応可能であるという意見が国際社会に広まりつつある、さらなる証拠であると見ています。

　17歳という若さで国王の座についた父は、絶対君主制国家の元首としてその責任の重さを痛感しました。しかし、国民が父の能力に全幅の信頼をおいていたために、在位当初でも父は摂政会議に補佐されることも出来ませんでした。将来に待ち受けている問題について評価していく中で、父は、過去10年以上にわたる計画的開発と近代化の結果、自分の国が変化しつつあることに気がついたのです。変化の中には、誇るべきものもありましたが、先が思いやられるような傾向にはこころを痛めました。当時、国内で進行中の開発が、本当に自国民を真の幸福へと導くのかということに、迷いを感じました。父は、国民の最も深い願いを知りたいという思いから、国中をくまなく旅し、国民と親密に触れ合う中で、市民一人一人にとって最も重要な願いは「幸福」であるという確信に至りました。それより大事なものはありませんでした。そ

こで、父は、国家の開発の目的は、個人、コミュニティ、そして国家的レベルで幸福を増大することであると考えて、それを実現する最適の方法を探し求めました。

　父は、既存の開発モデルが、いずれも互いに異なることを主張していますが、基本的には同じであることを発見しました。いずれの開発モデルも、幸福を目指すどころか、幸福がその目的であることを認識していませんでした。いずれのモデルも、全体的で、持続可能で、意味のある仕方で開発の理論的枠組みを提供していません。開発はより高い経済成長を求め続けるものであるという考え方に導かれて、すべての開発モデルは、国内総生産（Gross Domestic Product, GDP）を上げることにより、物質的な生活水準を向上させることを目指しています。しかし、幸いなことに、近年この世界的指標に、補足として失業、社会保障、社会基盤、法による統治などの指標も追加されています。これらの全ての指標は、市民の健康、安全、知的向上などにとって、非常に重要かつ基本的なものですが、それは、経済成長が促進されることによって、社会的、生態的犠牲をともなうことを無視しています。同様に、経済成長の恩恵が市民の間でどのように共有されるべきであるかについては、あまり真剣に考えられていません。つまり、豊かになるものが少しいたとしても、それによって目に余るような不平等が生じれば、社会全体としての健全性と長期的な持続可能性が、いずれは下降してしまうということは、既存の開発モデルにおいて考慮の対象ではないのです。

　既存の開発モデルの最も大きな欠陥の一つは、人々にはこころとからだの両方の成長に同じだけのニーズがあるということを認識していないことです。GDP誘導型のモデルでは、個人的かつ集団的な幸福をもたらすのに、最も基本となる、精神的、感情的、そして心理的ニーズが取り上げられていません。国王陛下は、特に人間の文明の産物であり、人間の価値の表現である文化と伝統が、通常の開発計画に盛り込まれていないことを懸念されました。それらが、個人のアイデンティティーと自尊心の確立には欠かすことの出来ない

ものである一方、社会の団結を促進し維持し、真の人間の発展を推し進める際に文化と伝統とが果す役割は、ほとんど評価されることはありません。その代わり、欲望、生き残り、競争といったあさましい本能を解き放つことによって、商業的価値観に基づく開発は、人間を飽くなき消費と浪費をする力を持つエコノミックアニマルに変身させるのです。近代工業社会の生命力として現在の市場を煽っているものは、まさにこの人間性の喪失なのです。

より多くのものを獲得し、蓄積し、消費するための競争は、すでにこの地球が生命を維持するための能力を低下させてしまっています。より多く、より早く、より優れた「商品」の需要は、ものすごいスピードでこの星の枯渇しつつある資源を取り出す巨大な機械群によって、効率的大量生産システムを生み出した技術革新の奇跡によって応えられています。ますます危険な物質の浪費と環境汚染が、その直接的結果です。水資源は枯渇しつつあります。ヒマラヤ山脈でも、極地においても、雪や氷が解けだし、その結果、海面が上昇しています。母なる自然が乱用され、不安定になれば、世界規模での自然災害が多発し、自然が荒廃することは、当然の結果であるように思われます。

最近になって、経済的発展を強調する開発モデルに内在する非常に深刻な欠陥によって、経済破綻が起こり、結果として一連の地域的または世界的レベルでの財政危機が引き起こされました。最近おきた経済ショックの結果、何百万もの人々が、仕事、家、そしてこれまでに蓄えた貯金を失い、最も伝統ある金融機関のいくつかが破綻寸前まで追い込まれました。私たちは、最悪の状態が終わった兆候を必死になって探し続けています。

世界は未だかつてこのような短期間に、これほどたくさんの説明し難い経済危機に陥ったことはありません。同様に、自然もこれほど多様な形で、これほどまでのスピードで、人間に対して猛威をふるったことはありません。未だかつて私たちの社会において、これほどまでにたくさんの命が自然災害によって失なわれたことはありません。最も貧しい国々においては、せっか

くこれまで築き上げてきた基本的な生活水準を低下させるなど計りしれない損害を与えています。さらに、これでも十分ではないと言わんばかりに、私たちは今おそいかかる、最も苦痛に満ちた災害に備えなければなりません。それは、経済的かつ生態的荒廃の累積効果の結果、襲いかかる社会的危機です。

　近い将来起こりそうな社会的災害について、今日私たちが見ることの出来るたくさんの兆しの中に、多元的な社会的貧困の中で富が上昇するというパラドックスがあります。世界が空前の繁栄と豊かさで満たされている中で、より多くの人々が絶望的な貧困に喘いでいるのです。すべての国々がますます軍事的に強くなっていくとき、国民は不安と恐怖の中で生活をしています。希望を求めて犠牲と困難を乗り越えて民主主義国が生まれていくにもかかわらず、自由と平等はただの願望だけにとどまっています。世界がますます小さくなり、都市化が進み、人々がますます狭いスペースにひしめき合って住んでいる中で、孤立、別離、寂しさは、ますます多くの人々の日常の現実になっています。中でも、意味のある人間関係が築けない、またはそれが存在しないことから生じる鬱病が、今日最も人々を苦しめる病気として蔓延していることも不思議ではありません。実際に、一年の中で、家族やコミュニティがその絆を祝いあうシーズンに、最も多くの人々が寂しさのせいで自殺を図っています。これらは、私たちの文明が物質的に豊かになるために、精神的、情緒的、そして人間関係の保全を代償として失くしてしまったことの証拠です。より多くの富を求める競争関係と、ほかの誰よりも自己自身を重要視することによって、家族、コミュニティー、そして社会のシステムまでも壊しつつあるのです。

　より多くの思想家、科学者、政治家や、企業のリーダーたちそして、一般庶民たちも、人間社会がさらによくない状況に向かっており、その存在自体が危機に瀕していることに同意しています。私たちはやり方を変えなければなりません。GDPに対する脅迫観念から抜け出す必要があります。私たちは心底から欲望をコントロールし、真の幸福を向上させることを願い、それを

総体的で持続可能な方法によって追及する必要があります。こういった考えが、私の父にこのGNHの理念を着想させたのです。したがって、このように急務を要する状況の中で、今世界がGNHの徳目を開発のための基本設計の新たな選択肢として注目しはじめたことは、全く理にかなったことではないでしょうか。

　国民総幸福による開発の理念、これは、国民の心の奥に秘められた願望に対する私の父の答えであり、二、三世代の物質的な便利さと繁栄のためだけにこの地球を略奪する、見境のないやり方に対する父の不満の表明でもあります。GNHは、人生そのものの意味と目的について熟考し、従来型の知恵にチャレンジする、父の勇気を示しています。父は、国民の集団的幸福を国家の目標として宣言し、その目的の追求を促進することが、国家統治の最優先事項としました。GNHは幸福追求を可能にする諸条件を作り出すこと以上の開発の目的はありえないという信念に基づいています。それは、さらに、幸福とは物質的快適さを得ることと、平和で正しく持続可能な環境の中で心と精神が成長することとの間のバランスを保つことによってのみ実現するという理解の上に成り立っています。GNHとは永続性のある幸福を見つけるものであり、他者の幸福の犠牲によって成り立つものではありません。それは人生をより充実させるものです。それには競争が全ての成功の基盤であるという考え方とは反対に、人間が相互に助け合う調和のとれた社会を築く方法を見つけることです。幸福とは、単に物質的な快適さではなく、人生の目的そのものであり、価値があり達成可能な目標であるという真実に、いつも心を向けなくてはいけないのです。それは決して禁欲主義でも、現実否定でもありません。ここで、国王陛下のお言葉をご紹介いたします。

「私は、今日のGNHとは、親切さ、平等性、人間性という根本的価値観と経済的成長を追求する必要性との間の橋渡しをするものであると信じる。」
　ブータン王国における幸福の追求は、最も広いレベルで、一般に四つの柱として知られている以下の四つの目標を同時に追求することであります。ブータ

ンの全ての社会・経済的プログラムは、わが国の若い民主主義の政治的発展を含めて、これらの柱の強化を認めるものでなくてはいけません。

　その四つの柱とは、
　　1）　持続可能にして平等な社会・経済的発展
　　2）　自然環境の保全
　　3）　文化振興
　　4）　すぐれた統治の強化
であります。

　これらは、1970年代以来、わが国の開発理念の核となる目標であります。しかし、GNHに対する世界の関心の高まりと、我々が住んでいる定量的な世界状況は、消費主義や個人主義という強力な行動規範に対抗して、GNHがより広く受け入れられ、用いられるべき、GNH指標の開発を促すことになりました。そのためには、学者達がGNHを深く研究し、社会的変化を導くGNH

の価値観を普及させるための研究に熱中できるようにする必要があります。経済専門家には、GNHの価値観を、求めるべき実質的富として定義し、普及させ、測定することを納得させなくてはいけません。さらに、社会を啓発し、人々がこれらの価値観を求めたくなるようにしなければなりません。政策立案者達に、人々に幸福の享受をもたらすこと以上の財やサービスはないということに気づかせなければなりません。

　真の富と繁栄とは、回復力のある環境の中で人間の生活を洗練し、未来を予測可能でより安全なものにし、コミュニティーと家族の絆を強くするものでなければなりません。GNHの富の創出は、協力、社会資本、そして人々の満足を促進するものでなければなりません。決してウォール街で追求されている、幻のようなつかの間の富であってはならないのです。GNH指数を開発するにあたって、四つの柱はさらに細かく九つの領域に分けられ、それは人間生活のすべての面を反映するようになっています。そのすべてが個人と社会の総体的な発展に不可欠であると考えられています。しかしながら、GNHは文化の柱に最も多い四つの領域を持たせていることを強調しておかなくてはいけません。このように、文化がブータンにおける幸福の主たる推進力として位置づけられていることは、明らかです。これら九つの領域と四つの柱の対応は以下の通りです。

　第一の柱を形成するのが「生活水準」「健康」「教育」です。
　第二の柱を築いているのが「生態系の健全性」です。
　第三の柱を構成するのが「文化」「精神的な幸福」「時間の活用」「地域社会の活力」です。
　第四の柱は実質的に「すぐれた統治」（民主主義、平等、正義）であります。

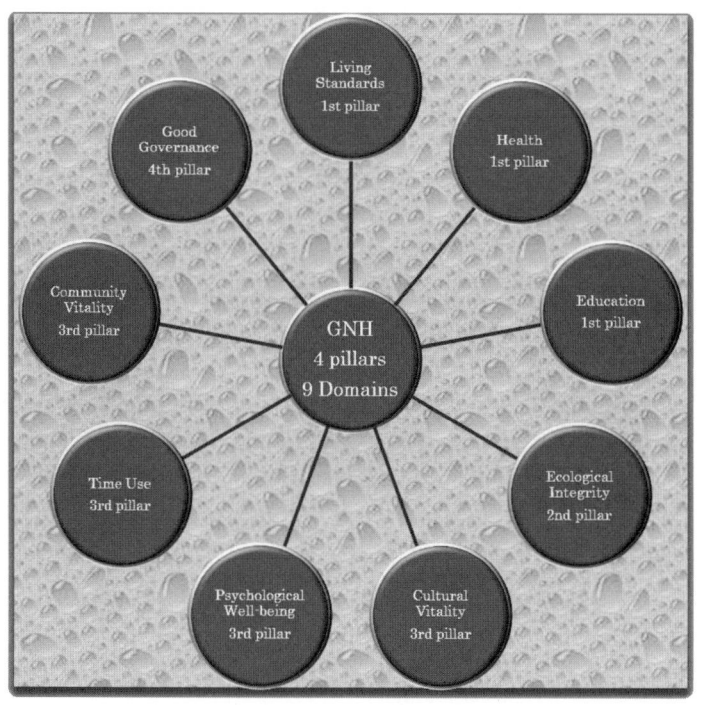

　これらの九つの領域は、さらに 72 の変数、または指標から成り立っています。ブータンはすでにこの包括的な指標を使い始めています。調査は二年ごとに行われ、すでに二回の調査が完了しています。調査結果は公開され、それを基に公共政策や社会計画に改善が加えられ、社会資本を配分するための指針として使われています。2008 年に行われた第一回目の調査では、精神の健全性を高め、ストレスを緩和し、心の活力を養ってくれる瞑想を定期的に行っているのは、ブータン国民の 3％にしかすぎないことがわかりました。この結果、現在すべての学校に瞑想を導入しました。さらに、新しい政策を「スクリーニングする」手続きも確立し、実施前にその政策が GNH の価値観にふさわしいかどうかを確認しています。

　ブータンの GNH の実践は、今までのところ実り多きものとなっていま

す。父の33年にわたる統治の期間は、しばしば黄金時代と呼ばれていますが、この間、ブータン王国はすべての分野において、かつてない発展を成し遂げることができました。これは国連人間開発指数においても最もよく反映されており、ブータンの人間開発度は「低」の位置から、「中」の位置にまで上昇しました。所得の面でも、世界の最貧国の位置から中所得国へと上昇したのであります。経済的尺度ではかることのできる進歩において、もっとすぐれた成功をおさめた国は他にあります。しかし、最も注目すべきことは、私達が文化的・社会的・政治的、そして生態系的対価をほとんど払うことなく、先に述べたような成果を達成できたということです。むしろブータンは幸福の追求を可能にするのに重要な領域において実際に進歩した、数少ない国と言うべきであるかもしれません。

　今日のブータンは、ほとんど本来の状態の自然環境を維持していることを自負することができます。それは環境問題が深刻な地球的規模の問題となる遥か前から環境保全に尽力してきたからであります。憲法で森林が永続的に国土面積の最低60％を占めるよう維持することが決められています。実際、今日のブータンでは緑地面積が国土の72％以上を占めています。そのお蔭で、他の同じ地理的条件下で見られるよりも、はるかに豊かな生物の宝庫となっています。ブータン人の生活様式の基本である文化と伝統は、このグローバル化した地球村の一員となった今でも、ますます繁栄しています。我々はさまざまな国際的フォーラムに信念を持って参加することにより、多くの友情と励ましを勝ち得てまいりました。父の数多くの功績の中でも、最も顕著なのは、2008年にブータン王国を最も若い民主主義国家に転換したことであります。父はこのように生涯の大望を成し遂げ、53歳で国王の地位から退かれました。偶然にも、この退位の行われた直前の国勢調査は、王国の国民の97％が幸福であることを明らかにしたのであります。このことにより、ブータンは開発の代替モデルとして、関心を持たれるようになったのであります。

　2008年はブータンにとって歴史的な年でありました。ワンチュック王朝

の百周年、第5代国王陛下の即位式、そして憲法制定をお祝いしました。この神聖な文書は、ブータンが永遠にGNHを追求することを保証するものであります。憲法には「国家は国民総幸福の追求を可能にするための諸条件を促進することに邁進する」と記されています。GNHに深く献身的に取り組んでおられる国王陛下は、国民総幸福は価値を伴った発展であるとしばしば仰せられています。さらに陛下の戴冠式のスピーチでも、このお考えを表明されています。

「我々の最も重要な目標は、国民の平和と幸福である。精神的に気高い国の国民として、あなた方はよき人間性を大切にする。すなわち、正直さ、親切さ、慈善の心、誠実さ、団結力、私達の文化と伝統の尊重、そして国を愛する心など。よき人間であるという簡明で時代を超えた目標を追求しつづけるかぎり、すべてのよきことを支持する国を建設する努力をつづけるかぎり、我々の子孫も何百年もの間、幸福で平安に暮らすことができるであろう。」

国王陛下は、国王として、国民をいかなる時も絶望させないことによって、民主主義のもとですぐれた統治を支持し補完しなければならないと、強く信じておられます。そのために陛下は、国中の社会的弱者をモニターし支援するためのネットワークを設立されました。私も含めて、王家のメンバーは、この取り組みに参加しています。死に向かう地球、経済の破綻、さしせまる社会的危機という現実に直面し、総体的な開発の枠組みとしてGNHが魅力的な提案として受け止められています。既に、GNHに関する、五つの国際会議が開催されました。先進諸国からなるOECDでは、一連の地域的もしくは世界的規模の会議を開いて、真の人間の進歩のための経済以外の方策の可能性を模索しています。オーストラリア、カナダ、中国、オランダ、タイでは、人間の幸福追求を、真剣に公共政策の中に取り上げています。英国では、保守党政権の下で総合的幸福（General Well-Being, GWD）を量るための調査を、この春から四半期ごとにおこなうことが決定されました。サルコジ大統領は、

GDPの支配に反対するチャンピオンになるべく挑戦しています。また、ブラジルでは、子どもたちを先頭に熱心なGNH信奉者がいて、上院では幸福を基本的権利として認めることが決定されました。ノーベル賞受賞者を含む著名な経済専門家たちも、幸福の追求に公共政策作成の焦点をあてることが効果的だと考えています。

昨年、ブータンは、ニューヨークで行われた国連MDG（Millenium Development Goal）サミットで、第九番目のミレニアム開発目標に、幸福を含めることを提案しました。それは、幸福が、貧しい国や発展途上の加盟国に関わる問題であるだけでなく、富める者も貧しい者も、すべての人類が時代を超えて結ばれる、共通のビジョンになると確信しているからです。意識的に幸福を求めることによって、人類の最善の性質が花開くでありましょう。そのような目標を追求することによって、私達の物質的な要求と、同じように重要な人間の他の要求や自然の限界を調和させる理性と才能を見出すことができるでしょう。これこそが、地球上の生命を持続可能にするものです。私達は、国家がいかにこの目標を追求するかが、その国の人々の真の幸福をどこまで真剣に考えているかの真の尺度となると確信しています。

では最後に、一つの考えを皆様におあずけしたいと思います。多くの国々と同様に、日本は経済的繁栄の頂点に到達したことで、これからは経済の低成長と高齢化社会という未来に立ち向かわなければなりません。そのような時代には、解決が困難な様々な問題を突きつけられ、創意工夫と勇気ある行動が求められます。しかし、他の国々と同様に、往々にして、慣れ親しんだ見方に留まり、従来と同じ型にはまった対策を講じるだけで済ませようという誘惑にかられます。たとえそれがよくても一時的な効果しかなく、長期的にはより危険であるとわかっていてもです。ただし、私は、日本が、もちろん世界全体もそうしないといけませんが、必ずや変化することを、そしてそれは日本独自のやり方で変わっていくであろうことを確信しています。その際、恐れながらも、GNHの理論的枠組みが、新しく再活性化された日本、真

の繁栄と幸福に満ちた日本の姿を心に描くために有用なアイデアを提供するのではないか、という提言をさせていただきたく存じます。私は、日本が、より幸せで持続可能な生活に世界を導くための、勇気と才能を持ち合わせていることを確信しています。

　ご清聴ありがとうございました。

　（文責　鍋島直樹・桂紹隆）

パネルディスカッション

コーディネーター
三谷 真澄（龍谷大学国際文化学部教授）

　ケサン・チョデン・ワンチュック王女殿下には龍谷大学においでいただき誠にありがとうございます。今回コーディネーターを務めさせていただきます、国際文化学部の三谷真澄と申します。私は仏教学・仏教文化学を研究しており、チベット仏教文化圏にも大変関心を持っております。ブータンはご承知のようにチベット仏教文化圏の一つでありまして、大乗仏教を国教とする唯一の独立国であると紹介されたり、世界有数の、「信仰密度」の高い国だと説明されることもあります。ブータン王国が大変信仰深い仏教国であるということは皆様もご承知のとおりでございます。

　私は2000年にパロ・ツェチュというブータン最大の祭りを見学し、西ブータンを何か所か訪問いたしました。私が訪れた国や地域の中で、一番好きな国の一つでございます。ブータンはGNHという新しい指標を提言されたことで欧米では高い注目を集めております。資本主義社会における閉塞感、経済的豊かさでは満たされない、人間の幸福のありかたに対する新たな提言、それをふまえた森林保護や環境政策という点からも大変注目を集めているところでございます。

近年ブータンは、テレビ番組等でも多くとりあげられるようになりましたので、ご承知の方もあるかと思います。TIME 誌で、毎年「世界で最も影響力のある 100 人」というものが発表されています。その 2006 年のリストのなかにこのたび表彰されました第 4 代国王が入っておられます。今回、さきほど若原学長の言葉にもありましたように、「KYOTO 地球環境の殿堂」入りの表彰式が行われ、王女であらせられますケサン・チョデン・ワンチュック殿下にお越しいただいたということは大変有り難いことであります。ブータン王国の世界的な知名度もますます増していくことと思います。

　これからの時間は王女殿下のご講演をうけまして、アジア仏教文化研究センター長の桂紹隆先生、人間・科学・宗教オープン・リサーチ・センター長の鍋島直樹先生から、今日のご講演に関するコメントと質問をいただき、それを受けてヴェツォプ・ナムギャル大使、カルマ・ツェテーム GNH 委員会長官よりお答えいただきたいと思います。

レスポンス
桂　　紹隆（龍谷大学アジア仏教文化研究センター長・文学部教授）

　それでは準備いたしました質問をする前に、王女殿下、素晴らしいご講演をありがとうございました。心から感動いたしました。特に最後のコメント、即ち日本の将来に向けての可能性についてお言葉をいただきましたこと、本

当に素晴らしいことだったと思います。実際にGNH政策が実践されている国の王女様から、日本の国民に直接お言葉をいただけたことは意味深いことだと思います。心から感謝申し上げます。

ケサン王女様、このたびは父王のご名代で「KYOTO地球環境の殿堂」の表彰をうけられましたこと、心からお祝い申し上げます。また、ただ今はブータン王国の仏教思想に基づく「国民総幸福 Gross National Happiness」の政策に関するご講演を賜り有難うございました。

最近我が国では「国内総生産 Gross Domestic Product」が中国に追い抜かれるということが大きなニュースになりました。1945年の第二次世界大戦敗戦後、戦争によって荒廃した国土の復興と国民生活の向上を願って我々はひたすら経済的発展を目指して参りました。その結果、ある程度公平な富の再分配と良好な治安状態を達成したのであります。急速な経済開発は深刻な公害問題を引き起こしましたが、その結果、経済的な先進国の間では最も意識的に環境問題の解決に取り組んできたと思います。

したがってGNHの4本の柱のうち3つの課題につきましては、我が国も完全ではありませんが、ある程度の成果を挙げてきたと思っております。しかしGNHの第3の柱である「文化・伝統の保護／精神的価値の保護」に関しましては、戦後日本は実質的には何ら積極的な政策を展開してきたとはいえません。歌舞伎や能などの伝統的芸能、大相撲などのスポーツは保護されてきたとしても、最も重要な精神的価値の保護については何ら積極的な政策は取られてこなかったと思います。

その背景には、日本国憲法で厳格な政教分離の原則のもとに、一切の宗教教育が禁止されているということがあると思います。その結果、精神的価値の保護の中心的役割を担うはずの家庭や家族の崩壊が、我が国がいま直面している最も重要な問題であると考えます。その意味でブータン王国のGNH政

策から我が国が学ぶべきことはたくさんあると確信いたしております。

　龍谷大学は昨年4月より、「アジア仏教文化研究センター」を立ち上げ、アジア諸地域における仏教の多様性とその現代的意義の総合的研究を行っております。アジアの諸地域を3つに分け、インド亜大陸と東南アジアを研究対象とする「南アジア班」、ブータンやモンゴルを含めた広い意味でのチベット文化圏と西域諸国を対象とする「中央アジア班」、そして中国・朝鮮半島・日本を対象とする「東アジア班」がございます。我々はアジア全域に広まった仏教の、各地域における展開の歴史を跡付けることにより、仏教の多様な実態を明らかにすると同時に、そのような多様性を可能にした仏教の寛容性の原理を世界に発信したいと思っております。さらに、現在アジアの各地域で行われている仏教の実態を調査し、21世紀の世界において仏教が果たしうる役割を明らかにし、日本仏教の活性化に寄与したいと思っております。

　そこで最後に王女殿下或いはお二人に質問がございます。
　ブータン王国は仏教を国教としておられますから、その「文化・伝統／精神的価値」の中心は仏教であろうと想像いたします。仏教王国ブータンの学校教育の分野で現在的な精神的価値、即ち仏教精神を子供たちに伝えるためにどのような宗教教育が行われているのかお教えいただければ幸いであります。よろしくお願い申し上げます。

コメント
V．ナムギャル（V. Namgyel ブータン王国大使）

　ありがとうございます。まず冒頭に、このような機会を与えてくださったことを龍谷大学の皆様にお礼申し上げたいと思います。私どもブータンでは、仏教は国教として存在しています。私たちがどのように子どもたちへの教育を行っているのか知りたいとのことでした。

　現在、私どもの学校では、具体的に仏教文献を教材として教えることはありません。しかし、仏教はブータンの人々の「生きる道」であります。ブータンの人々は皆仏教の中に生まれ、家庭の中で両親から仏教を学び、仏教は小さいときから私たちの文化、生活の一部なのです。人々は、仏教の価値を家族、特に両親から学びます。そして仏教教育を専攻したいと望む人は、国の助成を受けた仏教教団に入ります。そのほか、非公式の機関があります。これは国の直接の助成を受けているわけではありませんが、様々な先生から指導を受けることができるわけです。

　一方、通常の学校教育の中で、私たちは、現在なお仏教的価値を奨励しています。先生の責任で、特に国語（ゾンカ語）を教えるときに、そのゾンカ語クラスのなかで仏教的な考え方が教えられます。国語の教材に仏教の考え方が盛り込まれているからです。従って子供たちは小さい時から仏教的価値に触れながら成長していきます。私たちは、このことを続けていきたいと思っ

ていますし、拡大したいと思っています。そして、僧たちもまた、教団から外へ出て、ブッダが説き示した仏教的価値が人々の指針と成ることを人々にもっと広めていかねばならないと認識しています。

　生徒が成長する過程で、仏教的価値である「中道（middle path）」をあゆみ、正しい思考、正しい行動ということを学ぶ機会が必ずあるようにしなければなりません。ブータンの生徒、若い人たち、そして大人にも、中道によってバランスを維持していくことで、最も重要なのは、正しい思考、正しい態度、正しい行動だということを教えていきたいと考えています。ありがとうございました。

コメント
カルマ・ツェテーム（Karma Tshiteem　GNH委員会長官）

　ありがとうございます。このような機会をいただいたことを龍谷大学の皆様に心から感謝申し上げます。

　今、大使がおっしゃったことを少し補いたいと思います。宗教的営みという点で、この日本と同様に私たちも「政教分離」という考え方を持っています。公共政策というものはやはり公共の場の諸問題を取り上げるものでありますし、宗教は個人の問題でありますので、同じように政治と宗教を分ける考え

方はあります。しかしGNHを教育の現場に導入するという点で、多くの取り組みが私たちのすべての学校で取り入れられています。それほど新しいものではありません。例えば、毎日、学校が始まる前には集会があり、その集会は祈りから始まるのです。それは仏教の祈りです。

　また、GNHを考える際には、政策に落とし込む際、それはただちに宗教的ではないかもしれませんが、仏教による十分な影響があります。私たちの王は宗教的王、あるいは法の王であると考えます。王様たちのこの国に対する考え方やヴィジョンの持つ価値観に、仏教の影響は非常に大きいと思われます。

　学校では祈りのほかに、基本的に、普遍的な価値、すなわち、親切さ、慈悲、思いやりなどをこれまで教えてきました。GNHを教育に盛り込む前に、子供が先生を尊敬することを強調してきました。しかし、GNHを教育に盛り込んでからは、先生は、子供たちに、ただ尊敬の価値を教えるだけでなく、自分の振る舞いで尊敬という価値の模範となるようになりました。
　そのため、現在の学校では、昔と比べると先生と生徒の間の対話が変わってきたということがいえます。先生は生徒に対して尊敬を持って話をし、生徒は先生を模範として先生に尊敬をもって接するという相互関係ができていると思います。私たちの仏教によって与えられた重要な価値が、子どもたちに与えられています。

　また、王女殿下も先ほどの講演で強調されましたが、近年瞑想が学校に取り入れられています。瞑想は、子どもたちが静寂を経験するために導入しました。私たちは、彼らが大人になってもこれを覚えていてそれが、まさにライフスタイルの一つとなることを望んでいます。なぜなら、成長して大人になりますと、どうしてもストレスや競争の世界に入っていかなければなりません。瞑想によって、精神の糧となり、ストレスを緩和することができます。このすべては仏教的なものです。私たちは仏教的瞑想に影響されているからです。子どもたちは、瞑想を通して仏教の先生たちの事を思い出すでしょう。

したがって、私どもにとっては、仏教は、明確に中心的な役割を果たしています。しかし、同じ事を異なる場面で実践される場合には、単に特定の対象への精神集中と言った意味での瞑想であるかもしれません。ありがとうございました。

レスポンス
鍋島 直樹（龍谷大学人間・科学・宗教オープン・リサーチ・センター長・文学部教授）

ケサン・チョデン・ワンチュック王女殿下、こんにちは。ケサン王女殿下のお父上、ブータン王国第四代の国王陛下、ジクメ・センゲ・ワンチュック前国王におかれましては、「KYOTO地球環境の殿堂」を受賞なさいましたこと、誠におめでとうございます。ブータン王国の皆様が、地球環境の保護、生物多様性の保全に今まで貢献されてきたことを心から尊敬いたします。また本日は、龍谷大学において、ケサン王女殿下より、ブータン王国のGNH政策に関する特別講演を賜り、心から感謝いたします。王女殿下の講演を聞いて深く感動しました。

ケサン王女殿下のご講演にレスポンスするご縁をいただきありがとうございます。自己紹介をすることをお許しください。私は鍋島直樹と申します。龍谷大学教授、人間・科学・宗教オープン・リサーチ・センター長として、本学で仏教の思想、特に、平和と非暴力、あらゆるいのちへの慈悲と寛容さ

について講義しています。龍谷大学は仏教、特に日本浄土教の親鸞聖人の精神に基づいて建てられた大学です。「真実を求め、真実に生き、真実を顕かにする」、それが親鸞聖人による建学の精神です。他との関係性なくして存在するものはない、そうした縁起の真理に照らしてみると、自己中心的な生き方、排他的なあり方を反省し、他によって生かされているという自覚と感謝と謙虚さをもって生きることが大切であることに気づかされます。

私はブータン王国が大好きです。ブータン王国は、ダルシン（Dhar Shing）という経文が印刷された薄い布地が風にはためいています。どこまでも美しい田園風景と山々がつづいています。素晴しい光景です。とはいえ、まだ行ったことはないのですが、ぜひ行ってみたいです（笑）。

私はケサン王女殿下が紹介されたブータン国の法律に深い感銘を受けました。なぜなら、2008年に制定されたブータン王国の憲法が仏教の真理に基づいているからです。精神的財産について、ブータン王国の憲法第三条には、こう明記されています。

「仏教はブータンの精神的財産であり、なかでも平和、非暴力、慈悲と寛容の原則と価値を推し進めるものである。」

さらに、GNHの理想は、2008年に制定されたブータン王国の憲法の第九条にもこう明記されています。

「ブータン国は、国民総幸福の追求ができるように必要条件を推進することに尽くす。国は、虐待、差別、暴力から自由になる市民社会をつくり、この法律に基づいて、人間の権利と尊厳の保護、そして人々の基本的権利と自由を確保するように努めなければならない。」

世界中の人々は、ブータン王国のGNH政策に高い関心を寄せています。ブー

タン第4代国王ジクメ・センゲ・ワンチュック国王陛下は「国民総幸福（GNH）は、国民総生産（GNP）よりも重要である」と宣言しました。また、前国王は次のように発表しました。

「従来の開発モデルは、究極の目標として経済成長を強調している。GNH（国民総幸福）の概念は、物質的発展と精神的発展が互いに補完しあい強化するように並んで行われる時に、人間社会の真の開発がうみだされることを礎にしています。GNHの四つの柱は、「持続可能で公平な社会経済開発」、「文化的価値の保護と推進」、「自然環境の保全」、そして「良い統治の確立」である。」

GNH指数には四つの柱がたてられています。そしてこの四つの柱はさらに九つの領域に分けられ、人の生活のすべての面を反映しています。すべてが個人と社会の全体的発展に不可欠であると考えられています。特に、文化の柱には最大の四つのドメインがあることです。すなわち、文化がブータンの主たる推進力として位置づけられていることが明らかです。これら九つの領域とその柱について、
　第一の柱を形成するのが、生活水準、健康、教育、
　第二の柱を築いているのが、生態系の健全性、
　第三の柱に含まれるのが、文化の活力、精神的な幸福、時間の活用、地域社会の活力、
　第四の柱に含まれるのが、すぐれたガバナンス、すなわち、民主主義、平等、正義です。

私は、仏教は、縁起の真理に基づいていると理解しています。縁起とは大乗仏教において、あらゆるものが相互に依存し、関係しあっていることです。一つひとつの存在は相互に支えあう世界において、かけがえのない意味をもっています。ブータン王国では、この縁起の教えを尊重し、自己と他の一切の生命との関係性を尊重しています。自分の生命を尊重するとともに、他人の

生命を尊重しています。輪廻転生の見方は、生きとし生けるものが生まれ変わり死に変わりながら、家族であることを教えるものでしょう。だからこそ、他人を思いやり、森林を保護し、動物などのあらゆる生命を慈しんで生きることが、ブータンの人々にとって、功徳を積むことになると考えられていると思います。親鸞聖人も、「一切の有情はみなもて世々生々の父母兄弟なり」（『歎異抄』第五章）と語っています。自分ひとりだけの幸せを祈るのではない。相手の幸せを願うことが、ついには自己の幸せにつながることになるのではないかと思います。

　そこで、これに関連してお尋ねしたいと思います。ブータン王国の人々は、どのようなことが幸せだと感じるのでしょうか。縁起の真理、輪廻転生からの解脱という仏教思想と、GNHとはどのように関連しているでしょうか。

　私はケサン王女殿下の記念講演を聞いて、経済的な発展と心の豊かさとのバランスをとることが重要であることを再認識しました。伝統的な仏教文化を保護することは、心の豊かさにつながります。国民総幸福の理念は、仏教の中道の精神に基づいています。中道とは、両極端に偏らず、バランスをとりながら、心穏やかな道を歩むことです。

　歴史をふりかえってみると、日本の社会は、欧米に学び、勝れた科学技術を開発し、大きな経済的成長を遂げました。しかし一方で、日本は人類の経済的利潤を追求するあまり、生命の尊重を忘れ、地球環境も壊す結果を生み出しました。経済成長の陰で、自殺者もとても多いのです。21世紀に生きる日本の人々は、経済的にも精神的にも安らぎを感じることが少なくて苦しんでいます。

　真の幸福とは一体何でしょうか。わずかな人々が裕福になり、何世代もの人々の財産を独占することが本当の幸せなのでしょうか。一握りの人々の繁栄のために、世界の多くの人々の生活が犠牲になってはなりません。

ケサン王女殿下が提唱してくださったように、日本は経済的発展のみをめざすのではなく、国民総幸福の考え方を導入していくべきであると思います。一人ひとりのいのちが生き生きと輝き、人と人の絆を育み、心に幸せを感じることのできる世界を構築していくことが強く願われます。心の幸福と先端技術の平和的利用との両方が実現してこそ、日本は世界に愛される国となるでしょう。

阿弥陀仏の大悲の光にいだかれて、煩悩を離れることのできない自己を知ります。人は弱く、ひとりでは生きていけないからこそ、互いに許しあい、助け合って、世の安穏のために生きていくことができればと私は願っています。

ケサン・チョデン・ワンチュック王女殿下の美しい微笑みと明晰で穏やかな講演は、日本を包み込み、それは余韻となって今も心に響いています。
　ナミ　サミ　カディンチェラ。　どうもありがとうございました。

コメント
カルマ・ツェテーム（Karma Tshiteem GNH 委員会長官）

鍋島先生よりお心こもるレスポンスをいただきありがとうございます。先生と私たちは多くの深遠な考えを分かち合うことができました。先生がお尋ねになられた質問は、公共政策の構築という我々に与えられた仕事の範囲を大きく超えたものでありますので、私個人の見解としてお答えさせていただこうと思います。仏教の思想と国民総幸福の考え方は、私が先のコメントで明らかにしたように、「法の王」（Dharma King）と呼ばれている第四代前国王陛下が GNH を提唱されたのでありますから、それは明らかに仏教に影響されています。先のコメントで示した例からもお分かりのように、ブータン王国では、すべての分野において仏教からの影響を受けていることは疑いのない事です。それは、ただブータンの人々の生き方が仏教の影響のもとにある

からなのです。公的、私的をとわず、また文化と呼ばれるか伝統と呼ばれるかに関わらず、どのような儀式であっても、そのルーツは何らかの形で仏教の宗教的実践と関わりを持っています。そういう意味においては、ブータンのコンテキストにおいては、国民総幸福のためにすることは仏教と異なりませんし、仏教の影響を受けています。

すこし例をあげてお話したいと思います。最もよい例として皆さんにご紹介したいのは、現在の第5代国王陛下は、ブータン王国の全国各地を視察して、多くの子どもや学生たちと交流されます。それは子どもたちがブータンの未来を担うからです。国王陛下が国民総幸福について子どもたちと話しをされる時、実際、非常にシンプルなものの見方にしてお話しになります。国王陛下が生徒にいつもお尋ねになる質問は、「あなたは英雄になりたいか、それとも悪党になりたいか」と尋ねます。すると多くの子どもたちは英雄になりたいと答えます。すると国王陛下は「それはいいことだ」とお答えになるのです。私たちは人生においては常に選択をしないといけない場面に出くわします。そしてそこには2つの要素がいつもあります。一つは善につながる道、もう一つは悪につながる道です。そして、その選択の際には、善につながる選択でなくてはならないことを国王陛下は子供たちに考えさせるのです。

これは仏教思想の八正道に基づいています。（1）正見（真実の信知）、（2）正思惟（正しい内的態度）、（3）正語（正しい言語）、（4）正業（正しい行為）、（5）正命（正しい生活法、職業倫理）、（6）正精進（正しい努力、勇気）、（7）正念（正しい注意）、（8）正定（正しい瞑想、精神統一）です。そういう意味ではブータンで実践されている国民総幸福の考え方は非常に明らかに仏教に影響されていると思います。

またこのような例もあります。大きな企業は、GNHをビジネスにおいても反映させています。利益だけでなくそれ以外の要素も重んじます。そしてその他の要素を考慮する時には、バランス感覚が重要になりますし、また雇用

者や消費者の福利のために、ある程度の犠牲を払わなければならないことになります。このような実践の背景として働いている価値観は、他者のためをおもう慈悲という仏教の価値観があると言えるでしょう。つまり、先生のご質問に対するお答えとしては、我々ブータン王国の発展はGNH政策の影響を受けており、そしてそれは確かに仏教の価値観の影響の下で発展していると言えるということです。どうもありがとうございました。

コメント
V. ナムギャル（V. Namgyel ブータン王国大使）

　鍋島先生ご質問どうもありがとうございました。それでは、私はツェテーム長官の答えに少しだけ追加させていただこうと思います。鍋島先生よりブータン王国の人々にとって、何が幸せであるかという意味深い質問をいただきました。まず、ブータンの人々が人生の中で何を重要視しているかについては、統計によってその概要を知っていただければと存じます。私たちの国で、2008年に国民総幸福に関する国勢調査を行いました。人生において重要なものは何かを国民一人ひとりに尋ねました。まず一番目に、幸せのために「家族との生活」が大切であると95％の国民が応えました。二番目に、「責任感」が重要であると91.8％の国民が答えました。三番目に、「キャリアにおける成功」が重要であると90.3％の国民が答えました。そして四番目に、「精神的な信仰」が大切であると87.5％の国民が答えました。「財政的な安定」が重要であると87.5％の国民が答えました。そして「友情」は81.8％でした。「物質的な豊かさ」はその次でした。GNH政策においては「物質的な豊かさ」はあまり重要な事であると見なされていませんが、人々の間ではまだ非常に重要な事であると考えられているようです。79.8％の人がそれが重要であると答えています。この数字によってブータンの国民が何を幸福であると考えているか大体お分かりいただけるかと存じます。私たちが普及させようとしていることは、これらの要件のバランスを維持する事なのです。

また次に、仏教思想とGNHとがどのように関係しているかということについてもご質問いただきました。仏教とは中道の精神です。すべての仏教の伝統では、悲しみを取り除き、欲望を抑制しなければならないことを説きます。ではどうすればよいのか。その為に説かれるのが、中道ということであります。そして中道を歩みたければ、バランスを維持することが必要です。バランスを維持することにつきるのです。精神的な欲望、文化的な欲望、物質的な欲望の調和、融和であります。さまざまな欲望の融和を実現することができれば、地域社会の調和を維持することができ、国の調和を維持することができ、ついには世界の調和につながることができるでしょう。仏教思想はこのようにして我が国のGNHに貢献しているのだと理解しています。

　私たちは礼拝、祈りをささげますが、仏教によってその祈りは個人の利益ための祈りではないことを教えられるのです。寺院に行って仏に礼拝する時には、私たちの幸せがすべての生き物、すべての人々の幸せになるように祈ります。このように私たちは仏教徒としての実践を行い、GNH政策をすすめているのです。どうもありがとうございました。

コーディネーター
三谷 真澄（龍谷大学国際文化学部教授）

　すばらしいコメントをたまわりどうもありがとうございました。私ども龍谷大学は仏教系の大学でございますので、大変身につまされる思いで聞かせていただきました。まだまだ色々ご質問申し上げたいところでございますが、予定されている時間が迫ってまいりました。

　さきほどバランスということをおっしゃいました。いみじくもそのなかに仏教用語で「中道」と私たちが言っている言葉が出てまいりました。経済的発展と環境保全とはどちらかを優先してどちらかが犠牲となるようなものではなく、バランスの取れたものでなければならない。その政策の基盤は、仏

教の「中道」の精神にあったのです。

　また、経済的発展というものは、ある意味では、自分が、自分の家が、自分の国がと、自分のことを常に考えていくという側面があると思うのですけれども、一方で環境保全という、環境に対するなにがしかのアプローチというのは、常に自分以外のものに目を向けていく、つまり、他者に対する関心ということになろうかと思います。そういった意味で大乗仏教が目的としています自分自身へのメリットだけではなく他者に対するメリットを与え続けていくという、今日のご発表のなかには出てまいりませんでしたけれど、そういった側面が濃厚にあるように思います。本日のパネルディスカッションで、GNH政策の基盤になるところに仏教思想があるということがはっきりわかったような気がいたします。

　とかくGNH政策は、経済学や幸福論あるいは人類学など様々の側面から注目されておりますけれども、実はブータンの長い仏教文化の伝統が底辺にあることが見逃されているのではないか、そういうことを強く感じさせていただきました。

　今後もブータンはこのような仏教文化を基底とした社会を維持して、このまま進んでいっていただきたいと思います。そしていつまでも私の憧れであり、敬意を持ち続ける対象でいていただきたいと強く願っております。ちょうど時間となりました。どうもありがとうございました。

閉会の辞

赤松 徹眞（現龍谷大学第 18 代学長・文学部教授）

　ケサン王女殿下におかれましては、感動的なご講演をいただき誠に有難うございました。心から厚くお礼申し上げます。ご講演ではブータン王国のありようをご紹介いただきました。そこには広く仏教の教えがいきわたっている社会の豊さがあることを聞かせていただきました。大変感激をいたしました。

　私は先日、大橋照枝さんの『幸福立国ブータン』という本を読ませていただき、ブータン王国に関する予備知識を得ました。GNH（Gross National Happiness）は、ブータン前国王のジクメ・シンゲ・ワンチュック第 4 代国王が提唱されました。その後 2006 年にジクメ・ケサル・ナムギャル・ワンチュック皇太子が国王を継承され、2008 年に立憲議会制の民主主義国として発展をし、特にディクラム・ナムシャ精神というものを大切にされておられます。

　王女殿下のご講演にもありましたように、私たち日本は、相変わらずの経済成長一辺倒の社会という枠組みのなかに縛られ、いわゆる脱工業社会の展開に向けての社会像というのがなかなか描きにくく、私たちのなかには停滞感・閉塞感が漂っているような感じも致します。

そういった意味では、日本社会において人間や社会の豊さを育んでいく仏教の精神というものが徐々に希薄化していっているのではないか、随分と危機感をもたなければならないと感じさせていただきました。同時に私たちの龍谷大学においても大学を構成する学生或いは教職員の幸福度はどうであろうかと、このようなことを、ご講演をきかせていただきながら想い巡らしたことでございます。私は今、文学部長でありますけれども大学の運営に携わる者としては構成員の幸福度を想像して職務にあたらねばならないのではないかということを強く感じさせていただいたことでございます。

　今日ご講演をきかせていただいて、私も是非ブータン王国を訪ねさせていただきたいと思っております。その節にはお会いさせていただく機会がありましたらこの上なく幸いと思っております。

　ブータン王国の繁栄とケサン王女殿下のご健康を心から念じあげております。

　終わりになりましたけれども、会場の皆様方にはようこそご参加をいただきました。たくさんの方々が聴講をご希望になられましたが、教室事情でやむを得ずお断りしました方々には、申し訳なく思っております。ご参加をいただいた皆様方におかれましては今後の龍谷大学の発展にご支援ご協力を賜りますよう、また龍谷大学が展開していきます教育、研究、社会貢献という３つの分野にもご関心を寄せていただいてご協力をいただきたいと思います。またご講演にもありましたように幸福度ということで申しますならば、私たちは皆様方のお幸せを心から念じてご挨拶に代えさせていただきたいと思います。
　本日は誠にありがとうございました。

ブータン王国について

　ブータン王国（Kingdom of Bhutan）は、自国を「龍の国（ドゥク・ユル 'brug yul）」と呼び、国旗にも龍があしらわれている。その意味で、龍谷大学とは縁の深い仏教王国であるが、ここで簡単にブータン王国の概要を示しておきたい。

面積：約 38,394 平方キロメートル（九州とほぼ同じ）
人口：約 69.6 万人（ブータン政府資料 2010 年）
首都：ティンプー（Thimphu）
民族：チベット系（約 80%）、ネパール系（約 20%）等
言語：ゾンカ語（公用語）等
宗教：チベット系仏教、ヒンドゥー教等
以上は、2011 年 10 月現在。外務省ホームページ各国・地域情勢「ブータン」（http://www.mofa.go.jp/mofaj/area/bhutan/data.html）より抜粋

ブータンの概要

　チベット仏教文化圏は、チベットを中心に、東アジア文化圏・インド文化圏に匹敵する広大な地域に広がったが、19 世紀後半から近隣諸国、諸民族に併合・制圧されてしまった。そのような状況の中で、大乗仏教を国教として唯一独立を保って現在に至っているのが、ブータンである。

　ブータンは、大ヒマラヤ山脈東端の南麓に位置する小さな王国である。首都ティンプー（標高 2450m）は、1952～53 年に建設され、国際空港はパロ（標高 2500m）にある。ゾンカ語が公用語であるが、公式文書が英語で書

かれ、学校の授業は国語を除いて英語で行われ、『キュンセル』という最大の新聞も英語版が最も読まれているという。

ブータンと日本は、1986年に国交が樹立され、以後政府・民間レベルで友好関係が保たれている。中でも1994年に、日本政府が文化無償協力という形でゾンカ語タイプライターを供与したことは特筆される。

ブータンに早くからかかわった人物として、KJ法の創始者として知られる川喜多二郎氏（1920-2009）は、チベット文化圏のネパールを調査し、日本とブータンの友好に尽力した。西岡京治氏（1933-1992）は、ブータンで亡くなるまでの28年間農業指導に当たった。今枝由郎氏（1947-）は、フランス国立科学研究センターから派遣され、1981年から1990年までティンプーの「国立図書館顧問」として赴任した。

一方、1989年2月の大喪の礼に、当時34歳の第4代国王が参列し、翌年の即位の礼にも出席された。2011年11月17日には、31歳の第5代国王が国会演説を行われた。いずれも民族衣装である「ゴ」姿であった。

ブータン仏教略史

ブータンに仏教が伝来したのは、日本より1世紀遅く、7世紀前半のこととされる。チベット建国の英主ソンツェンガンポ王によって、全国各地に多くの寺が建立され、仏教を大いに広めたと言われるが、ブータン国内にも、西ブータン・パロ谷のキチュ・ラカン（仏像を奉った小さなお堂）と中央ブータン・ブムタン地方チョコル谷のジャンペ・ラカン等が、この王の建立にかかると言い伝えられている。

この仏教初伝から1世紀半経って、チベットではティソン・デツェン王が現れ、仏教を国教とし、仏教教団を設立した。この仏教導入に決定的な役割を果たしたのがパドマサンバヴァである。彼は、チベット・ブータン仏教で釈尊に次いで第二の仏と拝められるグル・リンポチェ（尊い師）の八相変化のひとつである。彼の信奉者はニンマ派（古派）とよばれる一大宗派を形成し、現在に至るまで、パロ谷のタクツァン、ブムタン・チョコル谷クジェ・ラカン等の数多くの縁りのある寺院がある。

11世紀になると、チベットではニンマ派に対して、サルマ派（新派）と総称される宗派がいくつも形成された時期であり、これらチベット仏教新旧各派は、南のブータンにも手を伸ばし始めた。そのうち最大勢力となったのが、西ブータンではカギュ派の一支派であるドゥク派で、中央及び東ブータンではニンマ派であった。このほかにも、いくつかの宗派があちこちの谷にその末寺を建立し、11世紀から17世紀までは、諸宗割拠の時代であった。

　この時代は、すべてチベット出身の高僧の活動が中心であったが、唯一の例外が、ペマ・リンパ（1450-1521）である。彼は、ある日グル・リンポチェの啓示を受け、湖の底に埋蔵しておいた経典や仏像を取り出した。以後彼は、埋蔵宝典発掘者（テルトン）として崇拝され、彼の教えはチベット・ブータンに非常に流布した。

　1616年、チベットのドゥク派の法主ンガワン・ナムゲル（1594-1651）は、自宗の信者が多くいる西ブータンに逃れ、57歳で寂するまでの35年間で、ほぼ現在のブータンをすべてドゥク派の下に統一し、政治的にもチベットから独立した。ドゥク派による政教一致体制で、ブータン全国に「ゾン」と呼ばれるドゥク派の寺院と政庁を兼ねた建物・組織が作られ、まとまりのある中央集権国家が誕生した。このゾンを中心とする行政組織は、現在のブータンにもそのまま生かされており、その意味でンガワン・ナムゲルは今でもブータン建国の父ということができる。

　彼の死後は、彼の化身活仏（シャプドゥン）を政治・宗教両面でのブータンの最高権力者とする体制が1907年まで続いた。この間、ブータンの南では、大英帝国がインド大陸を支配し、20世紀初頭にはヒマラヤを越えてチベットまで手中に収めようとしていた。この強力な外敵の脅威に対する危機感が、2世紀あまり続いた歴代シャプドゥンをめぐる内紛・内乱状態から、国内団結の気運を芽生えさせた。

　そこで、19世紀後半からブムタン地方に確固たる勢力を築き上げた一族の頭領ウゲン・ワンチュックを初代国王に選出し、世襲王制の下にブータンは改めて統一された。しかしながら実質は同一致体制の変革とも言えるもので、ドゥク派政教一体制が、同じドゥク派の政教二頭制になり、そのう

ち政治面担当の国王の権威が絶対的に強くなったと考えられる。

　ジクメ・センゲ・ワンチュック（1955-、1974戴冠）はこの世襲王制の第4代であるが、「大切なのは国民総生産（G.N.P.=Gross National Product）ではなく、国民総幸福（G.N.H.=Gross National Happiness）である」という語録（1972年即位演説、1976年など）に代表されるように、物質的発展による心の安らぎの喪失を憂慮し、伝統的文化と自然遺産を保存することにブータンの発展があるという信念のもとに施策がなされた。

　現国王は、第5代のジクメ・ケサル・ナムギェル・ワンチュック（1980- ）で、2006年12月14日に第4代国王が退位し、即日新国王として即位、2008年11月6日に戴冠式が行われた。ブータンは、立憲君主制・政党議会制民主主義の時代に入った。

仏教王国ブータン

　ブータンでは、民衆の日常生活の隅々にまで深く仏教が浸透しており、あらゆる面で仏教が規範・価値観を提供している。ゾンと呼ばれる首都及び各県の建物・制度は、国教であるドゥック派の僧院であり、かつ中央・地方の政庁である。

　全部で24ほどある祝日のうち、国体にかかわる、第5代国王誕生日（2月21〜23日）、5代国王戴冠記念日（11月6日）、第4代国王誕生日・戴冠記念日（11月11日）、王制記念日（12月17日）は西暦であるが、仏陀涅槃会（5月27日：2010年以下同じ）、グル・リンポチェ誕生日（6月21日）、仏陀初転法輪（7月15日）、仏陀降誕会（10月29日）、ティンプー・ツェチュ（9月17〜19日）等の仏教にかかわる祝日は、2月14日〜15日の正月（ロサ、ロサール）等とならんでブータン暦で行われるため、毎年変動する。

　全国・地方を通じて最大の祭りであるグル・リンポチェのツェチュ祭は、全国同じ日ではなく、各県ごとに日が異なっている。

ブータン仏教の特徴

　チベット・ブータンの仏教はさまざまな尊格のほかに、鬼神、精霊をもふくめたものである。これら一群の神・仏と信者との接点が、供養儀式であり、

法要である。ツェチュ（十日）祭は、最も重要なもので、グル・リンポチェの生涯における十二の出来事が、いずれも月の10日に起こったとされるところからこの名があり、彼は「月の十日に法要を勤める人のいるところには必ず戻ってくる」という言葉を残して、サンド・ペルリ（銅色に輝く山、師の本来の住まいである仏国土・極楽）に戻ったとする。

　そこでは、チャムと呼ばれる舞踊があり、特定の本尊や護法神を舞台の上に出現せしめる。これは仏教の儀式であり、説話の戯曲化であるが、その最終日の未明には、トンドルとよばれる大掛け物が開帳される。トンドルは、総絹アップリケ仕上げで、グル・リンポチェを主尊とし、両脇に二人の后、周囲にはグルの八相変化とかニンマ派、ドゥック派の高僧が配置してある。この仏画は「拝むだけで解脱が得られる」というご利益のあるもので、参拝者は、裾を額にいただき、祈りをささげる。仏画の前で厳粛な法要が営まれ、僧侶に布施がなされ、再びしまいこまれると、グル・ツェンギェ（グル・リンポチェ八相変化の舞）のチャムが演じられる。

　ブータン各地で、華麗にそして厳粛に繰り広げられるツェチュは、まさに仏教王国ブータンを象徴するにふさわしい祭りである。その最大のものが、パロ・ツェチュ祭で、ブータン暦2月11日から15日の5日間にわたって盛大に繰り広げられる。（西暦ではたいてい3月後半か4月前半の満月の日を最終日とする5日間であり、2000年は、3月20日が最終日であった。）

ブータン王家系譜図（一部）

第4代国王
ジクメ・センゲ・ワンチュック（1955-)
（アシ）ドルジ・ワンモ王妃（1955-)
　　……（アシ）ソナム・デチェン・ワンチュック王女（1981-)
　　……（ダショ）ジゲル・ウギェン・ワンチュック王子（1984-)
（アシ）ツェリン・ペム王妃（1957-)
　　……（アシ）チメ・ヤンゾム・ワンチュック王女（1980-)
　　……（アシ）ケサン・チョデン・ワンチュック王女（1982-)
　　……（ダショ）ウギェン・ジクメ・ワンチュック王子（1994-)
（アシ）ツェリン・ヤンドゥン王妃（1959-)
　　……**（ダショ）ジクメ・ケサル・ナムギェル・ワンチュック皇太子**（1980-)
　　　　　　　　　　　　　　　　　　　　　　　　→第5代国王
　　……（アシ）デチェン・ヤンゾム・ワンチュック王女（1981-)
　　……（ダショ）ジクメ・ドルジ・ワンチュック王子（1986-)
（アシ）サンギェ・チョデン王妃（1963-)
　　……（ダショ）カムスム・センゲ・ワンチュック王子（1985-)
　　……（アシ）ユフェルマ・チョデン・ワンチュック王女（1993-)

　　　　　　　　　※ダショ：王家・貴族の男性　アシ：王家・貴族の女性

ドルジェ・ワンモ・ワンチュック著・今枝由郎監修・鈴木佐知子／武田真理子訳『虹と雲―王妃の父が生きたブータン現代史』平河出版、2004の巻末「ヤプ・ウギェン・ドルジの系譜図」より抜粋（一部追記）

参考文献

- 赤瀬川原平『赤瀬川原平のブータン目撃』淡交社、2000
- 五木寛之『21世紀 仏教への旅 ブータン編』講談社、2007
- 今枝由郎『ブータンに魅せられて』岩波新書（新赤版）1120、岩波書店、2008
- 今枝由郎『ゾンカ語口語教本』大学書林、2006
- 今枝由郎『ブータン仏教から見た日本仏教』NHKブックス、2005
- 今枝由郎『ブータン中世史—ドゥク派政権の成立と変遷』大東出版社、2003
- 今枝由郎『ブータン—変貌するヒマラヤの仏教王国』大東出版社、1994
- 岩波書店「ブータン：〈環境〉と〈幸福〉の国」『科学』第81巻第6号（通巻946号）、2011年6月1日（今枝由郎、上田晶子、大橋力・河合徳枝、松島憲一、岩田修二・小森次郎、宮本万里、杉本均、坂本龍太、松沢哲郎他）
- 上田晶子『ブータンにみる開発の概念—若者たちにとっての近代化と伝統文化』（明石ライブラリー96）明石書店、2006
- NHK取材班『遙かなるブータン』ちくま文庫、1995（初版はNHK出版、1983）
- 大橋照枝『幸福立国ブータン—小さな国際国家の大きな挑戦』白水社、2010
- クンサン・チョデン・今枝由郎／小出喜代子訳『ブータンの民話と伝説』白水社、1998
- 佐々木高明『照葉樹林文化の道—ブータン・雲南から日本へ』日本放送出版協会、1982
- ジクミティンレイ著・日本GNH学会編『国民総幸福度（GNH）による新しい世界へ：ブータン王国ティンレイ首相講演録』芙蓉書房出版、2011
- 高橋洋（文・写真）『ブータン—雲の国の子供たち』大東出版社、1998
- 田淵暁（写真）・今枝由郎（文）『ブータン・風の祈り—ニマルン寺の祭りと信仰』平河出版社、1996
- ドルジェ・ワンモ・ワンチュック著・今枝由郎訳『幸福大国ブータン—王妃が語る桃源郷の素顔』NHK出版、2007
- ドルジェ・ワンモ・ワンチュック著・今枝由郎監修・鈴木佐知子／武田真理子訳『虹と雲—王妃の父が生きたブータン現代史』平河出版、2004

- 中尾佐助『秘境ブータン』毎日新聞社、1959（『中尾佐助著作集』第3巻）北海道大学国書刊行会、2005
- 永橋和雄（写真）・今枝由郎（文）『ブータンのツェチュ祭—神々との交感』（アジア民俗写真叢書12）平河出版社、1994
- 西岡京治・西岡里子『ブータン—神秘の王国』NTT出版、1998
- 平山修一『美しい国ブータン—ヒマラヤの秘境のブータンに学ぶ「人間の幸せ」とは!?』リヨン社、二見書房、2007
- 平山修一『現代ブータンを知るための60章』明石書店、2005
- ブータン王国教育省教育部編・大久保ひとみ訳『ブータンの歴史—ブータン小・中学校歴史教科書』（世界の教科書シリーズ18）明石書店、2008
- 宮本万里『自然保護をめぐる文化の政治 ブータン牧畜民の生活・信仰・環境政策』（ブックレット〈アジアを学ぼう〉16）風響社、2009
- 本林靖久『ブータンと幸福論—宗教文化と儀礼』法藏館、2006
- 山本けいこ『ブータン—雷龍王国への扉』明石書店、2001
- 山本けいこ『はじめて知るブータン』明石書店、1991
- レオ・E. ローズ著・山本真弓監訳・乾有恒訳『ブータンの政治—近代化のなかのチベット仏教王国』明石書店、2001

終わりに～編集後記

　この２月14日の講演において、ケサン王女殿下は、ヒマラヤの小王国ブータンの取り組みを威厳をもって表明され、そして同じ仏教国である日本の方向性を指し示して下さった。そのケサン王女殿下の優しいまなざしの講演を聴いてから１か月もたたない３月11日に、東日本大震災が起こった。その大震災に際し、世界中から心あたたまる支援が寄せられ、日本人は悲しみの中で支えあい、絆を大切にすることを学んだ。

　同年11月、ブータン王国第５代国王ジクメ・ケサル・ナムギェル・ワンチュック国王が新婚のお后とともに日本を訪問された。その目的は、東日本大震災の犠牲者とその家族に哀悼の誠を奉げ、被災地を訪問し、多くの寄附をされるためであった。11月17日には国会演説を行われ、日本への深い親愛の情と、日本人への最大限の敬意を表していただいた。この演説では、ケサン王女殿下の講演会と同じように、ブータンが仏教国であることに言及されず、仏教の術語も使用されなかったが、そこには確実に「仏教」の慈悲の精神が息づいている、そう感じたのであった。

　今回の出版物の基になる講演会は、最近特に話題となっているブータン関連の報道や、学術シンポジウムとは異なり、全面的に「仏教」色を押し出したものとなった。それは、親鸞聖人の精神を建学の基本理念とする、仏教系大学である龍谷大学にしかできないことである。誰もが精神的な幸福を忘れ、便利で安逸な生活に埋没し、経済的な繁栄以上の幸福の基準を持ち合わせることができないとすれば、それは大変悲しいことである。

　「幸福」とは、数値化できるものではなく、指標として明確な基準があるのかと問われれば、回答に窮するであろう。しかし、ブータン国民は確実に幸福である。ブータンに生まれ、ブータンで生活し、ブータンで死んでいくことが幸福であると考えている。そして何より、迷いから悟りへの道を志向する仏教に出遇えた幸福感が、彼らを支えているのではないだろうか。

　この出版物によって、私たちが本当の「幸福」とは何なのかを考え、日本の今後のあり方を考え直し、そして、今後ともブータン国民によって敬意を持ち続けていただけるよう不断の努力をしていく契機となれば、これに勝る幸せはない。

編集に際して、方丈堂出版に編成校正の労をお取りいただいたことに、甚深の謝意を表したい。
　最後に、ブータン王国のケサン王女殿下のご講演とご協力に、重ねて、心より深く感謝申し上げる次第である。

2012年2月18日

三谷 真澄

Acknowledgements

Her Royal Highness Pricess Kesang Choden Wangchuck, Princess of the Kingdom of Bhutan, visited Japan for the first time in February 2011 on behalf of her father, His Majesty Jigme Singye Wangchuck, the former King of Bhutan, who was then elected to the Earth Hall of Fame KYOTO. On this occasion Ryukoku University invited Her Royal Highness to deliver a lecture on the Gross National Happiness (GNH) policy of the Kingdom of Bhutan. The present volume contains not only Her Royal Highness' lecture "On Gross National Happiness: Bhutan's Development Philosophy" but also the opening and closing addresses by the former and present Presidents of Ryukoku University, as well as the Panel Discussion after the lecture, reproducing as faithfully as possible the whole event. We would like to sincerely thank Her Royal Highness Princess Kesang, who delivered a wonderful lecture, and His Excellency V. Namgyel, Ambassador of the Kingdom of Bhutan, and Mr. Karma Tshiteem, Secretary of the Gross Happiness Commission, who kindly participated in the Panel Discussion.

The present volume is published in both English and Japanese so that we can share with not only Japanese readers but also people around the world the successful results of the GNH policy of the Kingdom of Bhutan. We hope that this work might indicate one possible direction that may lead to the solution of problems the Earth is facing in the twenty-first century. On this occasion we would like to express our deep gratitude to the Kingdom of Bhutan as well as other countries in the world that have extended warm support to Japan after the great earthquake on March 11, 2011. We will be happy if readers facing our global crises and difficulties will reflect upon the importance of the GNH policy of the Kingdom of Bhutan.

Last but not least, we would like to thank the Kingdom of Bhutan and the Earth Forum KYOTO for their kind permission to publish Her Royal Highness' lecture, and Professor Kiichiro Tomino who made it possible to invite Her Royal Highness to Ryukoku University.

Name same kadrinche
Gasshō

Shoryu Katsura, Director of the Research Center for Buddhist Cultures in Asia, Ryukoku University
Naoki Nabeshima, Director of the Open Research Center for Humanities, Science and Religion, Ryukoku University

Opening Address

Dosho Wakahara, President of Chikushi Jogakuen University,
17th President of Ryukoku University

It is a great honor for Ryukoku University to be able to invite Her Royal Highness Princess Kesang Choden Wangchuck to deliver a special lecture during this year celebrating the 25th anniversary of the establishment of diplomatic relations between the Kingdom of Bhutan and Japan. The Kingdom of Bhutan is a world-renowned Buddhist kingdom. The Bhutanese government completed its transition to a constitutional monarchy in 2008 and is currently vigorously advancing the democratization and modernization of its society through the promotion of gender equality and information technology policies.

Since the 1980s, the Kingdom of Bhutan has employed the unique national development philosophy of Gross National Happiness, based not on gross national production but on Buddhist thought. Bhutan has demonstrated to the world that there can be a new vision of national development that fulfills people's happiness while respecting the harmonious co-existence of human beings and nature.

I have learned that Her Royal Highness Princess Kesang is the founder of the Gross National Happiness Centre. I am profoundly grateful to be able to learn about the GNH policy directly from her in today's lecture. According to the Ambassador of the Kingdom of Bhutan in Japan, His Excellency Mr. Namgyel, the Kingdom of Bhutan seeks to maintain a balance between economic development and spiritual happiness based on Buddhist teachings.

Scientific technology does not have a will of its own. It is humans who control scientific technology for meaningful purposes. However, there are no limits to human desires. It is religion's role to control human desires. From this perspective, our university advocates the integration of the humanities, sciences, and religion. Our university was founded based on the spirit of the teaching of Shinran Shonin, and for more than 370 years we have maintained the long tradition of the academic study of Buddhism. Among our research facilities, the Center for Humanities, Science, and Religion and the Center for Buddhist Cultures in Asia are developing extensive research projects that are supported by the Japanese Ministry of Education, Culture, Sports, Science & Technology. This special lecture has been made possible by the sponsorship of these two research centers, which aspire to share true academic values with the world.

I would like to thank everyone who has helped make this lecture possible today. It is a wonderful opportunity for Ryukoku University, established to promote the spirit of the Buddhist teaching, to have this special lecture by Her Royal Highness Princess Kesang of the Kingdom of Bhutan. I sincerely hope that this lecture will be beneficial to all our audience. Again I would like to express my deep gratitude to Her Royal Highness Princess Kesang.

Special Lecture

Her Royal Highness Princess Kesang Choden Wangchuck, the Kingdom of Bhutan

"On Gross National Happiness: Bhutan's Development Philosophy"

Her Royal Highness Princess Kesang Choden Wangchuck delivering a Special Lecture on February 14th, 2011, at Ryukoku University, Kyoto, Japan.

Introduction of the Lecturer

Her Royal Highness Princess Kesang Choden Wangchuck was born in 1982. She is the fourth daughter of the fourth King of Bhutan His Majesty Jigme Singe Wangchuck and the younger sister of His Majesty the King Jigme Khesar Namgyel Wangchuck, the current monarch.

Her Royal Highness attended public schools in Bhutan before pursuing a degree in psychology at Stanford University (USA). In 2007, she was appointed by His Majesty the King as His Majesty's Representative for People's Welfare in central Bhutan. Her Royal Highness is based in the district of Bumthang in order to effectively bring *kidu* (welfare) to the people. *Kidu* is a traditional duty of the King whereby those people who are vulnerable, and are out of the reach of mainstream development programs, are identified and granted assistance and support.

Her Royal Highness is highly committed to promoting the concept of Gross National Happiness both within the country and abroad and is the founder of the Gross National Happiness Centre established in Bumthang in central Bhutan.

Special Lecture by Her Royal Highness Princess Kesang Choden Wangchuck
On Gross National Happiness: Bhutan's Development Philosophy

It is with honor and pleasure that I bring to you the warm greetings of His Majesty Jigme Khesar Namgyal Wangchuck, the King of Bhutan. It is also my privilege to be the bearer of the message of good wishes from my father, His Majesty the former King, for the happiness of the Japanese people. My family and the people of Bhutan have always admired your great country for its achievement of the highest level of economic prosperity through innovation, industry and extraordinary harmony. And as a unique cultural entity and peace-loving nation, you are an inspiration to all other nations. I am therefore truly pleased to be visiting Japan for the first time and to have this opportunity to share with you the concept of Gross National Happiness (GNH) which was conceived by my father to put the Kingdom of Bhutan on a course of meaningful transformation. Bhutan is encouraged by your interest and sees it as a further sign of the growing belief of the international community in the relevance of our development experience to the larger world.

Having ascended the throne when he was barely 17, my father felt the full weight and enormity of his responsibility as the head of state and government of an absolute monarchy. Yet, vested with complete faith of the people in his capabilities, he did not have the benefit of a Council of Regency even in the early years of his reign. In assessing the challenges that lay ahead, he realized that his country was changing as a consequence of more than a decade of planned development and modernization. While some of the changes gave him reasons to be proud, he was troubled by certain trends that did not bode well. He wondered whether development as it was being undertaken would actually improve the true well-being of his countrymen. His enquiry into the deepest yearnings of his people led him to travel through the length and breadth of his kingdom, and his intimacy with the people convinced him that happiness is the singlemost important desire of every citizen. Nothing else mattered more. Having then understood that the purpose of national development must be the promotion of happiness at the individual, community and national levels, he searched for the most suitable means for its attainment.

He discovered that despite their claims to being different, all development models are essentially the same. None of them aspires for or even acknowledges happiness as a goal. None of them offers a paradigm for development in a way that is holistic, sustainable and meaningful. Guided by the notion that development is a continuous pursuit of higher economic growth, all of them aim to enhance material standards of living by raising gross domestic product (GDP). Fortunately, in recent years, this universal indicator is being supplemented by other yardsticks, which include unemployment, social services, infrastructure, and rule of law, among others. While all these are extremely important and essential to physical wellbeing, security and intellectual growth of citizens, they ignore the social and ecological costs at which growth is promoted. Likewise, no serious attention is given to how the benefits of economic growth are to be shared among the citizens. That, even as some prosper, gross inequities might eventually diminish society's collective wellbeing and long term sustainability, is beyond the concern of the development models.

One of the biggest defects of the conventional development models is their failure to recognize that human beings have equal needs for growth and development of the mind and the body. The GDP-led models do not address spiritual, emotional and psychological needs that form the primary basis for altering individual and collective happiness. His Majesty was especially concerned that culture and traditions, which are the products of human civilization and expressions of human values, usually find no place in development schemes. While these are critical to an individual's sense of identity and self esteem, their role in promoting and sustaining social cohesion and furthering true human development is largely unappreciated. Instead, by unleashing the baser instincts of greed, survival and competition, development with its commercial ethos is morphing human beings into economic animals with a voracious capacity to consume and waste. It is this dehumanization that now fuels the market, which has become the life force of modern, industrialized societies.

The race to acquire, accumulate and consume more has already diminished the capacity of our planet to sustain life. The demand for more, faster, and better "goods" is met through the miracles of technological innovation for efficient mass production systems that rely on gargantuan machines to extract with enormous speed the diminishing resources of the planet. Waste and pollution of the increasingly hazardous kind are the direct results. Water sources are drying up. The Himalayas and even the Polar Regions are shedding their snow and ice to cause rise in the sea levels. It seems only natural that as Mother Nature is abused and destabilized, she should react with what has become a global phenomenon of natural calamities of increasing frequency and devastation.

In recent years, the very severe flaws in the development models that emphasize economic development have caused the collapse of economies resulting in a series of financial crises at the regional and global levels. After the more recent and severe jolts, in which millions lost their jobs, homes, hard-earned savings, and the near collapse of some of the most venerable financial institutions, we are desperately looking for signs that the worst is truly over.

The world has never before suffered so many inexplicable economic crises in such a short time. Likewise, nature has never struck mankind with such fury in so many ways and with such rapidity. Never has it destroyed so many lives costing society incalculable damage including setting back nations from gains in the advancement of basic human conditions in some of the poorest countries. As if these were not enough, we must now brace ourselves for the greatest and most painful form of disaster that is already in the making. And I am referring to the social catastrophe that will strike as a consequence of the cumulative effect of economic and ecological devastations.

Of the many signs we see today of the impending social disaster is the paradox of rising wealth amid multi-dimensional societal impoverishment. More people are trapped in abject poverty as the world experiences unprecedented prosperity and affluence. As all nations become militarily stronger, their citizens live in the shadows of insecurity and fear. Freedom and equity remain mere aspirations even as more democracies are born from sacrifices and struggles for hope. As the world becomes smaller and urbanized and as people are crammed together into ever shrinking spaces, isolation, separation and loneliness are everyday realities for an increasing number of people. It is no wonder that today the biggest illness that plagues mankind is depression arising, among others, from failure or absence of meaningful relationships. In fact, it is during times of the year when families and communities ought to celebrate their cherished bonds that loneliness drives the largest number of people to suicide. These are indeed signs of our civilization having become materially richer at the cost of psychological, emotional and relational integrity. The rivalry for greater wealth and the importance of self over all else are destroying family, community and social systems.

A growing number of thinkers, scientists, political and corporate leaders as well as ordinary people agree that human society is doomed to face more and worse situations and that its very survival is at stake. We need to mend our ways. We need to get away from our obsession with GDP. We desperately need to control our greed, aspire for things that will raise our true wellbeing and pursue them in ways that are holistic and sustainable. These were the very thoughts that inspired my father into conceiving the philosophy of GNH. It therefore seems perfectly logical that the world, under compelling circumstances, is now beginning to see the virtues of GNH as an alternative development architecture.

The development philosophy of Gross National Happiness is my father's response to the innermost yearning of his people and his dissatisfaction with the reckless manner in which our planet is being plundered for the material convenience and prosperity of a few generations. It is a reflection of his courage to challenge conventional wisdom having pondered the meaning and purpose of life itself. He declared collective happiness the goal of our country and facilitating its pursuit the highest priority for his rule. GNH is based on the belief that there can be no higher purpose for development than the creation of enabling conditions for the pursuit of happiness. It is further founded on the understanding of happiness as a state of being that can only be realized by balancing gains in material comfort with growth of the mind and spirit in a peaceful, just and sustainable environment. GNH is about finding durable happiness, of the kind that does not come at the cost of the well-being of others. It is about making human life more fulfilling. It is about finding ways to build harmonious societies on mutually supportive human relationships as opposed to competition being the basis for all success. It is about having to be mindful of the truth that happiness, not merely material comfort, is the purpose of life and that it is a worthy and achievable end. It is certainly not about asceticism and denial. Here I quote His Majesty the King who said,

> I believe GNH today is a bridge between fundamental values of kindness, equality, and humanity and the necessary pursuit of economic growth.

The pursuit of happiness in Bhutan has been, at the broadest level, a concomitant effort to achieve four goals known popularly as the four pillars. All socio-economic programmes including political development of our young democracy must subscribe to the strengthening of these pillars, which are:

a. Sustainable and equitable socio-economic development,
b. Environmental conservation,
c. Promotion of culture, and
d. Enhancement of good governance.

```
            ┌─────────────────┐
            │  Sustainable    │
            │  and Equitable  │
            │  Socio Economic │
            │  Development    │
            └─────────────────┘
                    │
┌──────────┐    ┌───────┐    ┌──────────────┐
│Enhancement│───│  GNH  │───│ Environmental│
│ of Good  │    │   4   │    │ Conservation │
│Governance│    │Pillars│    │              │
└──────────┘    └───────┘    └──────────────┘
                    │
            ┌─────────────┐
            │ Promotion of│
            │   Culture   │
            └─────────────┘
```

While these are the purposes that form the core of our development philosophy since the late 1970s, the growing interest in GNH worldwide, and the quantitative world we live in have persuaded us to develop a GNH index so that it can find wider acceptance and application against the powerful ethics of consumerism and individualism. These include the need to enthuse academics into conducting deeper research and promoting GNH values to guide societal change; to convince economists to define, promote and measure these values as real wealth to aspire for; to create an enlightened society that will want to pursue these values; and to cause policy makers to realize that there are no greater goods and services for the people than those that facilitate their enjoyment of happiness.

Real wealth and prosperity must refine human life within a resilient environment; render the future more predictable and secure; and strengthen relationships within community and family. The generation of GNH wealth must promote cooperation, social capital and contentment. They must not be of the illusory or ephemeral kind promoted by Wall Street. In developing a GNH index, the four pillars have been elaborated into a total of nine domains, which represent all the dimensions of one's life. All are considered crucial to the holistic development of the individual and society. However, it must be underlined that the cultural pillar has the maximum number of four domains, making clear its position as the principle driver of happiness for Bhutan. These nine domains and the pillars to which they belong are:

a. Living standard, health and education that form the first pillar,
b. Ecological integrity that constitutes the second pillar,
c. Cultural vitality, psychological well-being, time use and community vitality that comprise the third pillar, and
d. Good governance (democracy, equity and justice) which is the substance of the fourth pillar.

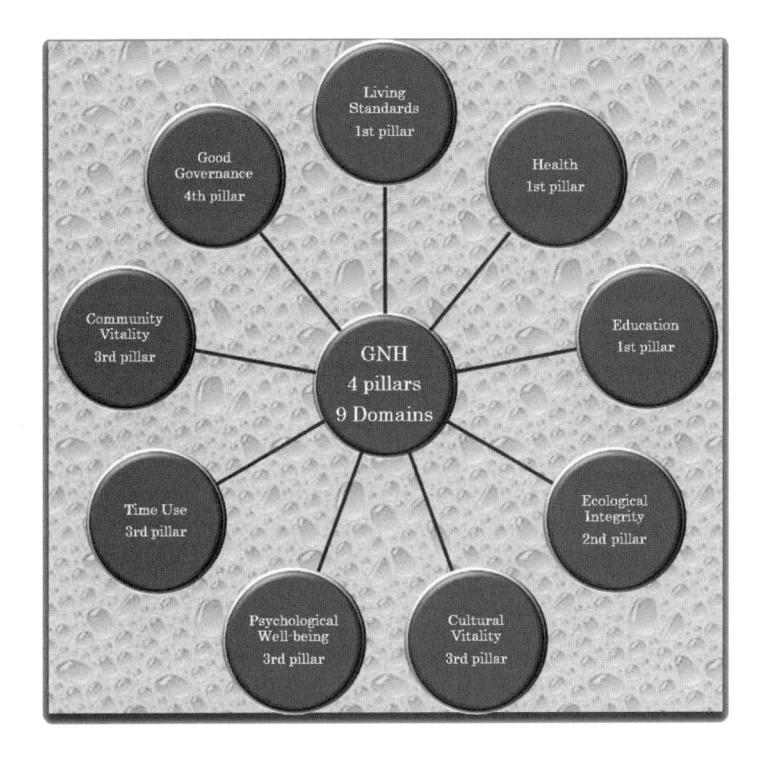

Each of these nine domains is made up of a total of 72 variables or indicators. Bhutan has already begun using this comprehensive index. Surveys are carried out once every two years, with two having been completed thus far. The findings, which are made public, are used to refine public policies and programmes and to guide resource allocation. The first survey carried out in 2008 showed that meditation, which enhances mental well-being, reduces stress and nourishes spiritual vitality, is practiced regularly by only 3% of Bhutanese. As a policy response, we have now introduced meditation in all our schools. Furthermore, procedures have been established to "screen" new policies so as to ensure that they subscribe to GNH values before they are implemented.

Bhutan's pursuit of GNH has, thus far, been rewarding. During the 33-year reign of my father, often referred to as the golden period, Bhutan witnessed unprecedented progress in all areas of development. This is best reflected in the UN Human Development Index where Bhutan moved from a Low Human Development status to the Middle Human Development level. In terms of income, Bhutan also rose from being among the poorest countries in the world to a medium income country. What is remarkable is not so much the progress against these yardsticks of which there are far better examples of success. It is the near absence of cultural, social, political and ecological costs at which our achievements have been made. In fact, Bhutan may be among the few countries where gains have actually been made in these spheres that are critical to enabling the pursuit of happiness.

Bhutan today can boast of a largely pristine environment thanks to our commitment to environmental conservation long before it became a serious global concern. With the constitutional commitment to maintaining a minimum forest cover of 60% in perpetuity, Bhutan today has an expanding green cover beyond 72%. This is complemented by an extremely rich bio-diversity that far exceeds what might ordinarily exist within any similar geographic space. Our culture and tradition—foundations for the Bhutanese way of life—are flourishing even upon having become a part of the globalized village. Our principled participation in the international fora has won us many friends and well-wishers. What will, however, stand out among the many great achievements of my father will be the transformation of the kingdom of Bhutan into the youngest democracy in 2008. Having thus achieved his life's ambitions, my father retired from his royal duties as the King at the age of 53 years. Incidentally, it was by sheer coincidence that a population and housing census which preceded his abdication revealed that 97% of the people in the kingdom were happy. These have made Bhutan a subject of interest in the context of an alternative development model.

2008 was a historical year for Bhutan, during which we celebrated 100 years of the Wangchuck era, the enthronement of His Majesty the Fifth King and the enactment of the Constitution. The sacred document ensures that Bhutan will forever remain devoted to the pursuit of GNH. It states that, "The State shall strive to promote those conditions that will enable the pursuit of Gross National Happiness." His Majesty the King who is deeply committed to GNH has often stated that, to him, Gross National Happiness is simply development with values. This was further reflected in his Coronation address.

> Our most important goal is the peace and happiness of our people. As citizens of a spiritual land, you treasure the qualities of a good human being—honesty, kindness, charity, integrity, unity, respect for our culture and traditions, (and) love for our country. ... As long as we continue to pursue the simple and timeless goal of being good human beings, and as long as we strive to build a nation that stands for everything that is good, we can ensure that our future generations for hundreds of years will live in happiness and peace.

His Majesty firmly believes that as King, he must support and complement good governance in our democracy by ensuring that people do not despair at any time. To this end, His Majesty has established a network that monitors and supports vulnerable groups throughout the country. Members of the Royal Family, including myself, are part of this effort. Faced with the realities of a dying earth, failing economies and an impending social disaster, GNH as a holistic development paradigm is being seen as an attractive proposition. Five international conferences on GNH have been held. The OECD, comprising the developed countries, has held a series of regional and global conferences in its search for a non-economic measure for true human progress. The Australians, Canadians, Chinese, Dutch and the Thais are taking the pursuit of happiness or human well-being seriously in their public policies. Britain has recently taken a decision to begin quarterly surveys starting in spring to measure General Well Being (GWB) under the Conservative government. President Sarkozy dares to be a champion against the dominance of GDP. In Brazil, there is a strong GNH following, with children in the lead and the senate having resolved to include happiness as a fundamental right. Notable economists, including noble laureates, also see the benefits of pursuing happiness as a focal point for public policy making.

Last year, Bhutan proposed the inclusion of Happiness as the Ninth Millennium Development Goal at the UN MDG Summit in New York. This is based on our conviction that as a goal, its relevance goes beyond the poor and developing member states to bind all of humanity, rich and poor, to a timeless common vision. It will be in the conscious pursuit of happiness that the very best in the nature of the human race will flourish. Through the pursuit of such a goal, we will find the reason and genius to moderate and harmonize our, otherwise, largely material wants with the other equally important human needs and nature's limitations. It is what will make life on earth sustainable. We are convinced that the way in which a nation pursues this goal will be the truest measure of its devotion to the promotion of its people's true well-being.

In closing, I would like to leave you with a thought. As with many countries, I believe that Japan, having reached the pinnacle of economic success, is now confronted with a future of slow economic growth and an aging population. Such times pose difficult challenges and call for ingenuity and daring. But, as in other countries, the temptation will be to remain on familiar grounds and to apply the same conventional solutions even though, at best, their effects will be temporary and, in the long run, even more hazardous. What I do know is that Japan will change as indeed the whole world must, and that it will do so on its own terms. In so doing, it is with deep humility that I suggest the GNH paradigm might offer useful ideas for the envisioning of a new and reinvigorated Japan, one that is truly prosperous and happy. I know that Japan has the courage and genius to lead the world into a happier and sustainable way of life.

I thank you for your kind attention.

Panel Discussion

Coordinator
Mazumi Mitani (Professor, Faculty of Intercultural Communication, Ryukoku University)

I would like to thank Her Royal Highness Princess Kesang Choden Wangchuck for visiting Ryukoku University. My name is Mazumi Mitani of the Faculty of Intercultural Communication, and I will be the coordinator for this panel discussion today. I study Buddhism, particularly its socio-cultural aspects, and I have a deep interest in the areas influenced by Tibetan Buddhist culture. Bhutan, as you know, lies within the sphere of Tibetan Buddhist cultural influence and is often introduced as the only independent country where Mahāyāna Buddhism is recognized as the state religion. Bhutan is often cited as a country with a very high "faith-density" in the world. It is very well known that Bhutan is a deeply religious Buddhist country.

In the year 2000, I had an opportunity to visit Bhutan to observe Paro Tsechu, the largest festival in Bhutan. During my trip, I also visited several sites in western Bhutan. Of all the countries and places I have been in the world, Bhutan indeed is one of my favorites. Bhutan's introduction of the new social growth index called GNH has increased people's interest in Bhutan in Europe and the United States, where there is a sense of the stagnation of capitalist society, that economic affluence alone is unsatisfying, and that we need a new way to approach human happiness that includes forest preservation and environmental policies.

In recent years many TV programs and other media have featured the Kingdom of Bhutan, so many of you may already be familiar with this country. For example, every year *Time* magazine makes a list of the 100 most influential people in the world. In 2006, the *Time* 100 included His Majesty Jigme Singye Wangchuck, the fourth King of Bhutan. And, as we heard in the message delivered by President Wakahara, it is our great honor to be able to receive Her Royal Highness Princess Kesang Choden Wangchuck, who attended the induction ceremony at the Earth Hall of Fame KYOTO on behalf of her father. We are now witnessing the increasing renown of the Kingdom of Bhutan in the world.

Now, in response to the lecture by Her Royal Highness, we will begin a panel discussion session. First, I would like to invite comments and questions from Professor Shoryu Katsura, Director of the Research Center for Buddhist Cultures in Asia, and from Professor Naoki Nabeshima, Director of the Research Center for Humanities, Science and Religion. Then we would be pleased to hear further comments by His Excellency V. Namgyel, Ambassador of the Kingdom of Bhutan to Japan, and Mr. Karma Tshiteem, secretary of the GNH Commission.

Comment and Question

Shoryu Katsura (Director of the Research Center for Buddhist Cultures in Asia, Ryukoku Univercity)

Your Royal Highness, before presenting my question, I would like to thank you for your wonderful lecture. I was indeed much impressed by your talk, especially your last comment on the possibilities for the future of Japan. I think that it is particularly important that we have heard this message directly from the princess of the country where the GNH policy is actually implemented. I would like to offer my deepest appreciation and thanks.

Princess Kesang, I would like to congratulate you on your father, His Majesty the former King of Bhutan, receiving this commendation from the Earth Hall of Fame KYOTO. And I thank you very much for delivering your speech on the policy of Gross National Happiness, which is based on Buddhist thought.

Recently in Japan it has been much reported that the Gross Domestic Product (GDP) of China has superseded that of Japan. Since 1945, the end of World War II, Japanese people have worked very hard to achieve economic development, wishing to rebuild the country that was devastated by war and to improve the standard of living.

As a result, we have achieved to some extent the fair redistribution of wealth among people and relatively good conditions of public welfare. Although rapid economic development also brought about the serious problem of pollution, as a result, we have been forced to solve environmental problems with a determination that may be marked highest among the economically developed countries.

Consequently, of the four pillars of GNH, I may say that we have somewhat accomplished three of them, albeit not perfectly. However, regarding the third pillar of GNH, which is the conservation of culture and tradition and the preservation of spiritual values, I do not think that post-war Japan has pursued any positive policy. The traditional performing arts such as Noh and Kabuki as well as traditional sports like Sumo have been well supported by the government. However, regarding the most important spiritual values, no positive policy has been created.

One of the main reasons behind such a phenomenon, I think, is the absolute prohibition of religious education in Japanese public schools because of the strict separation between religion and politics under the post-war Japanese constitution. As a result we are facing the most serious problem of the disintegration of the traditional family, which is supposed to play the most important role in the preservation of spiritual values. In this respect, I am convinced that there are many things we can learn from the GNH policy of the Kingdom of Bhutan.

In April of last year, Ryukoku University established the Research Center for Buddhist Cultures in Asia in order to study the historical diversity as well as the contemporary significance of Buddhism in Asian countries. We divided Asia into three zones, namely, (1) South Asia, covering the Indian subcontinent and Southeast Asian countries; (2) Central Asia, including the broad Tibetan cultural area such as Bhutan and Mongolia; and (3) East Asia, covering China, Korea and Japan. We intend to trace the historical development of Buddhism in order to clarify its diversity in various areas of Asia, and at the same time to send a message of religious tolerance, which makes such diversity possible, to the rest of the world. Furthermore, our research projects will study the contemporary situation of Buddhism in various areas of Asia in order to clarify its possible role in the 21st century world, and in this way we hope to contribute to the revitalization of Buddhism in Japan.

Now here is my question to Her Royal Highness, or to the two representatives of the Kingdom of Bhutan. Since Buddhism is the state religion of the Kingdom of Bhutan, the idea of 'culture and tradition' or 'spiritual welfare,' I think, mainly comes from Buddhism. Therefore, I would like to know what kind of religious education you are providing to school children in order to teach them traditional spiritual values, that is, Buddhist spiritual values, in the Kingdom of Bhutan.

Reply

His Excellency V. Namgyel (Ambassador of Bhutan, Royal Bhutanese Embassy)

Firstly I would like to say thank you for the opportunity to be here at Ryukoku University. Professor, as you said, we have Buddhism as the state religion in Bhutan. And you would like to know how we are educating our children.

Currently in our schools we do not specifically have Buddhist texts taught as a subject separately. But Buddhism is the way of life in Bhutan. We are all born into Buddhism with our parents and our culture. Right from childhood, Bhutanese people learn the values of Buddhism from their parents. And for those who want to specialize in Buddhist education, they can join the body of monks that is sponsored by the state. And for those who want to join other areas of Buddhist studies, we also have informal institutions which are not directly state-sponsored, but they can learn under different teachers.

But in the regular schools we still encourage Buddhist values in the way of life under the responsibility of the teachers, particularly the teachers who teach our national language in the Dzongkha classes, since in the Dzongkha classes the textbooks have Buddhist content in them. And because of that, our children grow up with Buddhist values in life right from childhood, and we would like to continue doing that. Also we would like to further expand that, and the monks are now also realizing that they should go out and give talks and let people know values taught by Lord Buddha which will guide the life of people.

We have to make sure that students as they grow older get the opportunity to exchange ideas and learn the values of Buddhism, which basically is there in following the middle path, particularly right thought and right action. This is what we would like to do, and we are trying to teach our students and young people and even adults in Bhutan that you follow the middle path to maintain balance in life.

And most important is right thought, right attitude and right action. Thank you.

Reply
Karma Tshiteem (Secretary, Gross National Happiness Commission)

Thank you very much. I would also like to thank the organizers for the opportunity to be here at Ryukoku University.

I would like to complement what His Excellency the Ambassador just said. In terms of what we are doing religiously, very much like here in Japan we also separate the religious space from public policy-making. Public policy obviously deals with the issues in the public domain and religion is something very much in one's individual space. So we do have a similar separation. However, as part of including GNH into education, we have a number of initiatives that have been introduced in all our schools. Some of the initiatives are not very new, but are built into the old. So for instance, we don't have religion as a subject, but everyday when school starts there is a school assembly, and at the assembly everything starts with a prayer. One can imagine that these are very much Buddhist blessings.

There is no denying that GNH in terms of the work we are doing to operationalize it into policies is very much areligious. But it is fully influenced by Buddhism. In many ways we consider our kings to be religious kings, or Dharma kings, and clearly all the values that they have shared in their philosophy and vision for the country are influenced by Buddhism.

Now in the schools, in addition to prayers, we have basically in the past been teaching very universal values of kindness, compassion, generosity, etc. The difference this time as part of including GNH into education is actually, instead of trying to teach children values of respect, the teachers are modeling that behavior themselves.

So today when we go to our schools, the interaction between teachers and students is very different from before. Teachers speak with respect to students, and in turn students realize the value of respect, which must always be mutual. These are some ways in which our important values influenced by Buddhism have been imparted to children.

Also, as Her Royal Highness highlighted in her address, we have introduced meditation. At the moment, the state of meditation is introduced as an activity for our children to experience stillness. We do hope, however, that as they become adults, they will remember this and that it will become part of their life style, because, you know, as you grow up you enter the competitive world, and you are likely to feel stress, and meditation can be very good for spiritual nourishment and reducing stress. All this is in the Buddhist context, of course, because we are influenced only by Buddhist meditation. Most of our children, of course, then think of some Buddhist teachers. So in our case, clearly Buddhism has a central role. But if you do practice in another setting, it could just be meditation that just focuses on an object. Thank you.

Comment and Question
Naoki Nabeshima (Director of the Open Research Center for Humanities, Science and Religion, Ryukoku University)

Your Royal Highness Princess Kesang Choden Wangchuck, *kuzug zang pola*—congratulations—to your father, the fourth King of Bhutan, His Majesty Jigme Singye Wangchuck, for his induction into the Earth Hall of Fame KYOTO in 2011. We all deeply appreciate that the Kingdom of Bhutan has contributed to conservation of the global environment and biodiversity. I wish to thank you for the special lecture on Gross National Happiness in the Buddhist Kingdom of Bhutan that you gave today at Ryukoku University. I was deeply moved by your lecture.

It gives me great pleasure to have the opportunity to respond to your lecture. First, allow me to introduce myself. I am Naoki Nabeshima. I teach Buddhism, especially topics on nonviolence, compassion and tolerance, which, of course, is inclusive of the natural environment, as professor and director of the Open Research Center for Humanities, Science and Religion, at Ryukoku University in Kyoto, Japan. The university is a Buddhist-based institution of the Shin Buddhist School founded by Shinran (1173–1262) in Japan. "Seek for the truth, live in the truth and manifest the truth." This is the school motto of Ryukoku University. There is nothing that exists independently in itself alone. From this truth of interdependence, we learn that we must reflect on our egocentric, divisive tendencies and, with deepening awareness that we live dependent on others, grow in gratitude and humility.

I love the Kingdom of Bhutan. In pictures of Bhutan, I see so many *dhar Shing*, the small flags printed with Buddhist sutras, fluttering in the wind. Bhutan possesses beautiful rural landscapes and mountains. The scenery is wonderful. I have never been to Bhutan, but I would really like to visit Bhutan someday.

I am very impressed with the constitutional system of the Kingdom of Bhutan as introduced by Princess Kesang. The constitution established in 2008 is based on the truth of Buddhism. Spiritual heritage is spelled out in the Constitution of the Kingdom of Bhutan, Article 3.

> Buddhism is the spiritual heritage of Bhutan, which promotes the principles and values of peace, non-violence, compassion and tolerance.

Further, the pursuit of GNH is delineated in Article 9.

> The State shall strive to promote those conditions that will enable the pursuit of Gross National Happiness. The State shall endeavor to create a civil society free of oppression, discrimination and violence, based on the rule of law, protection of human rights and dignity, and to ensure the fundamental rights and freedoms of the people.

People around the world are very interested in Bhutan's concept of Gross National Happiness. The fourth King of Bhutan, His Majesty Jigme Singye Wangchuck, instituted GNH at the beginning of his reign in 1972. The happiness of the people was made the guiding goal of development. He stated, "Gross National Happiness (GNH) is more important than Gross National Product (GNP)." He also said,

> While conventional development models stress economic growth as the ultimate objective, the concept of GNH is based on the premise that true development of human society takes place when material and spiritual development occur side by side to complement and reinforce each other. The four pillars of GNH are the promotion of equitable and sustainable socio-economic development, preservation and promotion of cultural values, conservation of the natural environment, and establishment of good governance.

In the process of developing the GNH indexes, four pillars are established. These four pillars are further divided into nine domains reflecting all aspects of human life. All of these factors are considered necessary for the holistic development of individuals and society. Four of these nine domains—almost half—are within the pillar of cultural values. That is, clearly culture is recognized as the principal driving force for the development of Bhutan. Following is a list of the nine domains included in the four pillars.

1. The first pillar is formed of the domains of living standard, health, and education.
2. The second pillar consists of the domain of ecological integrity.

3. The third pillar comprises cultural vitality, psychological well-being, time use, and community vitality.
4. The fourth pillar is good governance (democracy, equality, and justice).

Buddhism is based on the truth of dependent origination. In Mahāyāna Buddhism, dependent origination means that all beings and things are mutually dependent. Each individual existence has an integral meaning in an interdependent world. In the Kingdom of Bhutan, this teaching of dependent origination is respected, and the relationships between oneself and all other living beings are also respected. Just as one respects one's own life, one likewise respects the lives of others. I believe that the Buddhist view of transmigration is a teaching that all things that live, perish, and are reborn, are our family. For this reason, I believe, the people of Bhutan think that such things as being considerate toward others, preserving forests, and compassionately regarding all living beings, including animals, are in themselves acts that create merit. Shinran, the founder of the Jōdo Shinshū tradition, also said, "In the past, all living beings have been our fathers and mothers, brothers and sisters, through countless lives" (*Tannisho*, 5). One cannot wish only for one's own happiness. Hoping for the happiness of others is itself what leads to one's own happiness.

In this regard, Your Royal Highness Princess Kesang, I wonder if you would be able to tell us, for the people of Bhutan, what kinds of things are considered to be happiness. And what is the relationship between Buddhist thought and Gross National Happiness?

Hearing Princess Kesang's special address, I realized again that it is very important for us to keep a balance between economic development and spiritual happiness. The preservation of traditional Buddhist culture brings spiritual growth. Respect for balance is based on the philosophy of the middle way in Buddhism. The middle way means that one does not lean toward extremes and takes a moderate way.

Looking back on our history, Japanese society, following the lead of European and American countries, has developed advanced scientific technologies and has achieved great economic growth. However, unfortunately, Japan has sought only an economic profit that benefits human beings, and the result has been that we have forgotten about respect for life and have destroyed the natural environment. There are also a great number of people who commit suicide. In Japan in the twenty-first century, both economically and spiritually, we rarely feel peace of mind, and therefore we suffer.

What is true happiness? Is becoming rich and monopolizing the fortunes of many generations true happiness? A great many people's lives in the world must not be sacrificed for the prosperity of a few rich people.

As Princess Kesang has proposed, people in Japan should not only seek for economic development. I believe that we should also introduce the philosophy and policy of Gross National Happiness. I very much hope that we can transform our world so that the life of each individual can shine brightly, strengthening the bonds among people, and we all can feel spiritually happy. By attaining spiritual happiness together with the peaceful application of scientific technologies, Japan would become a country respected in the world.

When I realize that I am embraced by Amida Buddha's light of compassion, I also realize that I cannot escape from my own blind passions. But it is my hope that, although human beings are weak and cannot live without each other, we can forgive each other, help each other, and work together for the peace and tranquility of the world.

I feel as if Her Royal Highness Kesang Choden Wangchuck's beautiful smile and brilliant lecture have embraced Japan, and even now it echoes in my mind.
Name same kadrinche la.
Thank you very much.

Reply
Karma Tshiteem (Secretary, Gross National Happiness Commission)

Thank you very much, Professor Nabeshima, for your rich response. I think there are many profound thoughts that you have shared with us. And I believe, for the type of questions that you have asked us, I will have to respond with my own personal views, since I think they are far beyond the type of work we are doing in public policy making. Basically, when it comes to the question about the relationship between Buddhist thought and Gross National Happiness, as I highlighted earlier, clearly this philosophy emanates from His Majesty the Fourth King, whom, as I said, we consider as a Dharma King. Clearly it is influenced by Buddhism. There is no doubt, as you can see in the examples that I gave earlier, what we do in Bhutan is very much influenced by Buddhism in every respect. And that is simply because the Bhutanese way of life is strongly influenced by Buddhism. In any ceremonies, whether they are official or private, or whether we call them as our culture or tradition, actually, their roots are always something to do with Buddhist religious practices. So there is no doubt that in the Bhutanese context, what we do for the Gross National Happiness is no different from Buddhism and is influenced by Buddhism.

Now, as an example, I think the best example that I can share with you is that, when His Majesty the King is going around the country, he always takes time to meet with students, the children, who are the future of Bhutan. And when he speaks to them about Gross National Happiness, he actually distills it into very simple points of view. One of the questions he always asks the student is, "Do you want to be a good person, to be a hero? Or do you want to be a villain?" And most of the time, the response from the children is that they want to be heroes. And he says that's good. In our life, in everything you do, at every moment, you are faced with choices that you have to make. And this choice always has two elements. One will be a good way and the other will be a bad way. And you must always stay on the good way.

Clearly, when I look at this, it is deeply influenced by Buddhist values, the ideas of right thought, right action, right livelihood, right meditation, and so on. So, I think Bhutan's Gross National Happiness and what we practice in Bhutan are very clearly influenced by Buddhism.

There are other examples that I could share with you. Even among our corporations, some of our large corporations are incorporating GNH into the way they do business. Now when they started doing this, they immediately had to move beyond the bottom line of profits to include other considerations. When they began considering other factors, then they found that they had to maintain a good balance and give something in some sense, make some sacrifice even in the bottom line, to watch out for their employees or for the welfare of consumers. So if we deconstruct this, the underlining value here is again the Buddhist value of compassion, making consideration for others. So I would like to say that, in response to your question, in the way that our development has been influenced by Gross National Happiness, it is no different from the influence by Buddhist values. Thank you very much.

Reply
His Excellency V. Namgyel (Ambassador of Bhutan, Royal Bhutanese Embassy)

Thank you, Professor Nabeshima, for your profound questions. I would like to supplement Mr. Tshiteem's response to these questions just a little bit. You asked what kind of things are considered to be happiness for the people of Bhutan. Statistically, I would just like to give you a little idea of what the Bhutanese people find very important in their life. In 2008, we did a survey asking people what they consider to be very important in their lives. Number one was family life. 95% of the people considered family life to be very important in their lives. Number two was a sense of responsibility. 91.8% of the people gave that response. Then number three was success in career. 90.3% considered that this was very important. Then number four was religious faith. 87.7% of the people considered this to be very important. Then comes financial security. 87.5% of the people considered it very important. Then, 81.8% of the people considered that friendship is very important. Then came material wealth. Gross National Happiness does not mean that material wealth is not important. It is important for quality of life, and 79.8% of the people considered it to be very important. This gives a rough idea of what Bhutanese people consider to be important for happiness. So that's what we are striving to promote, to maintain the balance of these.

The next question was about the relationship of Buddhism to GNH policy. What is the relation? Buddhism talks about the middle path. All Buddhist traditions propagate that the best thing is to get rid of suffering, first by getting rid of desire. But how do we do that? We have to follow the middle path. If we follow the middle path, it means maintaining balance. It's all about maintaining balance. Maintaining balance between material aspirations, spiritual aspirations, and cultural aspirations. If you maintain harmony in all this, you maintain harmony in society. If you maintain harmony in society, you maintain harmony in your country. If you maintain harmony in your country, you help to promote harmony in your region and the world.

So this is how Buddhism contributes to GNH for our country. And when our people pray, we are taught to pray not for the benefits for individuals. When we go to temples, we pray so that our prayers and wishes may benefit all sentient beings, and of course, all human beings. This is how we follow Buddhist practice and GNH. Thank you.

Coordinator
Mazumi Mitani

Thank you very much for your wonderful comments. Because Ryukoku University was originally founded on the spirit of Buddhist teaching, I can very well empathize with all your comments. I think there are still many questions and comments, but unfortunately our scheduled time is almost up and we must close our discussion session.

During our discussion, we talked about balance in connection to the Buddhist concept of the middle way or middle path. We cannot give priority to either economic development or environmental conservation. We cannot accomplish one by sacrificing the other. We need to maintain a balance of both development and conservation. And we learned that at the foundation of GNH lies the Buddhist teaching of the middle way.

When we talk about economic development, we tend to see development only from the side of ourselves, for our own families, or for our own country. On the other hand, when we think about environmental conservation, or any type of approach to environmental issues, we need to consider others as well. We need to become interested in the existence of others. So we must not only seek for merit for ourselves, but provide merit to others, which is the ideal of Mahāyāna Buddhism. This is very important and was also expressed in the lecture given by Her Royal Highness about GNH and in the comments made by His Excellency Ambassador Mr. Namgyel. By participating in today's discussion session, it has become very clear to me that Buddhist thought is the foundation of the GHN policy.

Currently, many scholars are interested in studying GNH policy from various academic fields, such as economics, the study of the theory of happiness, and anthropology. But I also strongly feel that we often forget that at the root of the GNH policy there is a long tradition of Buddhist culture in the Kingdom of Bhutan.

I sincerely hope the Kingdom of Bhutan will continue to maintain its society based on Buddhist culture. As such, Bhutan will always have our admiration and respect. Thank you very much.

Closing Address
Tesshin Akamatsu (Professor, Faculty of Letters, 18th President of Ryukoku University)

Your Royal Highness Princess Kesang Choden Wangchuck, thank you very much for your wonderful presentation. From the bottom of my heart, I would like to say thank you so much. Your presentation has introduced the Kingdom of Bhutan, and I am very impressed to learn of the spiritual wealth of this society that is deeply influenced by the teachings of Buddhism.

A few days ago I read a book titled *The Kingdom of Bhutan, A Nation Founded on Happiness* by Ms. Terue Ohashi. From that book I was able to get some idea about the situation of Bhutan. In the presentation by Her Royal Highness Princess Kesang Choden Wangchuck, we learned that GNH was introduced by His Majesty the fourth King Jigme Senge Wangchuck. In 2006 Prince Jigme Namgyel Wangchuck succeeded to the throne, and in 2008 the nation became a constitutional monarchy in which the spirit of *driglam namzha* (traditional etiquette) is especially respected.

As was also mentioned in Her Royal Highness' address, in the case of Japan we still maintain the same old model obsessed with economic development, and being trapped in this system and unable to envision how to move toward a post-industrial form of society, we have a sense of stagnation and despair.

In this sense, the spirit of Buddhism that has engendered the flourishing of Japanese society is now becoming hard to find. With today's presentation, I have been made aware that we should have a strong sense of alarm about this fact. As I listened to the talk, I also thought about this university, Ryukoku, and I could not help but wonder what is the level of happiness of our students, faculty, and staff. I was strongly made aware of the fact that, as the current dean of the Faculty of Letters it is my responsibility to consider the happiness of our community as part of my duties in running the university.

After hearing today's lecture, I hope that I will be able to visit Bhutan one day. It would be my greatest pleasure to have the opportunity to meet you again.

I offer my greatest wishes for the continuing prosperity of the Kingdom of Bhutan and the health of Her Royal Highness Princess Kesang.

In closing, I would like to say thank you to everyone for joining in this session. There were many more people who wished to attend, but due to space limitations we were unfortunately unable to accommodate everyone. My apologies for this. For those who have attended today, I hope we will have your continued support and cooperation in the future development of Ryukoku University. There are three areas in which we seek to develop the university—education, research, and contributions to society—and I do hope that you will be interested and support these efforts. In light of the idea of happiness that was in today's presentation, in parting, I offer you my sincerest wishes for your happiness.

Thank you very much.

Postscript

In this lecture, Her Royal Highness Princess Kesang Choden Wangchuck exlained with gravity the issues that face the small Himalayan kingdom of Bhutan and suggested possible directions for Japan, which is likewise a Buddhist country. Less than one month after Princess Kesang's gracious speech, on March 11, the Great Eastern Japan Earthquake occurred. As a result of this great disaster, Japan has received warm-hearted support from around the world, the Japanese people have supported each other in the midst of sadness, and we have learned the importance of the bonds that link people together.

In November of the same year, the fifth King of the Kingdom of Bhutan, King Jigme Khesar Namgyel Wangchuck, visited Japan together with his new wife the Queen. The purpose of his visit was to offer his sincere condolences to the victims of the disaster and their families, to visit the disaster area, and to make a large monetary contribution to the disaster relief efforts. On November 17, the King delivered an address to the Japanese Diet expressing his deep affection for Japan and his great respect for the Japanese people. In his address, as in Princess Kesang's lecture, he did not mention the fact that Bhutan is a Buddhist nation, nor did he use Buddhist terminology. But I felt nevertheless that in his words certainly lived the spirit of Buddhist compassion.

The special lecture that forms the basis of this publication is different from the media reports on Bhutan that have recently become popular, nor is it an academic symposium. Every aspect of this lecture highlighted the Buddhist flavor of Bhutanese culture. This is something that could only be accomplished at Ryukoku University, a Buddhist-based university with its founding principles based on the spirit of Shinran Shōnin. It would indeed be a sad thing if people were to forget the spiritual basis of happiness, becoming immersed only in lives of convenience and ease and unable to apprehend the basis of happiness beyond economic prosperity.

Happiness is not something that can be given a numerical value, and if one were asked if there is a clear standard by which it can be measured, one would be at a loss to answer. Yet the Bhutanese people are clearly happy. Being born in Bhutan, living one's life in Bhutan, and dying in Bhutan is itself happiness. Most importantly, the view of happiness encountered in Buddhism, which aims at a path leading from delusion to enlightenment, must certainly act as a support for them.

With this publication, we hope to consider what "happiness" truly is and to rethink the future of Japan. And if this were to become an opportunity for our continuing efforts to maintain the respect of the Kingdom of Bhutan, that would be our greatest happiness.

We would like to express our deep appreciation to Hōjōdō Shuppan for their assistance with the editing of this book.

Finally, I would like to express my deepest gratitude once more to Princess Kesang for her lecture and her kind cooperation with this publication project.

February 18, 2012

Mazumi Mitani

ケサン王女殿下特別講演 ブータン王国の国民総幸福(GNH)政策
　　　－仏教思想はどのように活かされるか－

2012年3月30日　初版発行

講　演：ケサン・チョデン・ワンチュク王女殿下
共　編：龍谷大学　アジア仏教文化研究センター
　　　　龍谷大学　人間・科学・宗教オープン・リサーチ・センター
発行者：光本　稔
発　行：株式会社 方丈堂出版
　　　　本社 〒601-1422 京都府京都市伏見区日野不動講町38-25
　　　　　　電話 075-572-7508 FAX 075-571-4373
発　売：株式会社 オクターブ
　　　　　　〒112-0002 東京都文京区小石川2-23-12
　　　　　　　　エスティビル小石川4F
　　　　　　電話 03-3815-8312 FAX 03-5842-5197

ISBN978-4-89231-095-9 C1015